Ghost Towns
of the
Santa Cruz Mountains

Ghost
Towns
of the
Santa Cruz
Mountains

John V. Young

Great West Books   Lafayette, California

Cover design by Larry Van Dyke
Cover photos by Peter Browning
Map by Michael Banta

Manufactured in the United States of America

Library of Congress Cataloging-in-Publication Data

Young, John V.
    Ghost towns of the Santa Cruz Mountains / John V. Young.
        p. cm.
    Originally published: Santa Cruz, Calif. : Western Tanager Press, 1984.
    Includes index.
      1. Ghost towns—California—Santa Cruz Mountains. 2. Santa Cruz
    Mountains (Calif.)—History, Local. I. Title.

F868.S33 Y68 2002
979.4'71—dc21

                        2002070003

Great West Books
P.O. Box 1028
Lafayette, CA 94549-1028
Phone & Fax: (925) 283-3184
E-mail: peter@greatwestbooks.com
http://www.greatwestbooks.com

Photo credits:
Alyce Marie Taylor, pp. 31, 34; William A. Wulf, pp. 18, 91; U.C. Santa
Cruz Special Collections Library, pp. 21, 22; Courtesy Carolyn DeVries,
p. 129; all other photos by the author.

To Emma Lou

my co-pilot and constant companion
during fifty-odd years
of delving in the boondocks

Other books by John V. Young

Contemporary Pueblo Indian Pottery
(with Francis H. Harlow), 1965, 1974

The Grand Canyon, 1969

*Hot Type & Pony Wire: My Life as a California Reporter
from Prohibition to Pearl Harbor*, 1980

*Kokopelli: Casanova of the Cliff Dwellers:
The Hunchbacked Flute Player*, 1990

The State Parks of Arizona, 1986

The State Parks of New Mexico, 1984

State Parks of Utah: A Guide and History, 1989

A page from the original "Ghost Town" newspaper series.

Contents

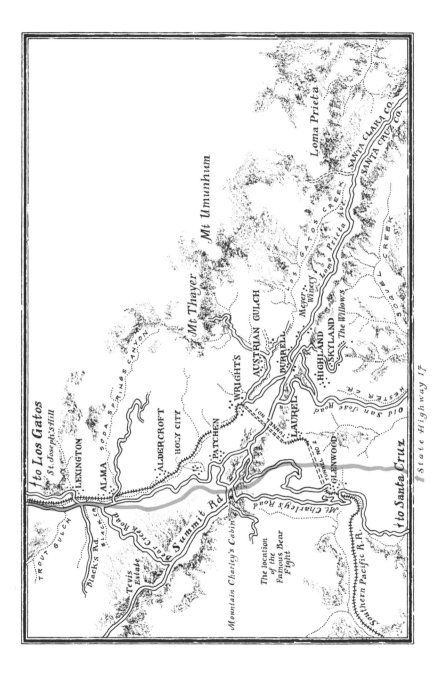

Preface
How the Stories Came to Be Written

Under the title "Ghost Towns of the Santa Cruz Mountains," these stories appeared in 1934 in the *San Jose Mercury Herald* as a copyrighted Sunday feature series. The series began April 22, and ran every Sunday until July 22. A final installment was published December 2, 1934.

I wrote the stories as a cub reporter covering a country beat that included Campbell, Los Gatos, Saratoga, and the adjacent foothills of the Santa Cruz Mountains, which I had known as a boy. My home was in the rural area between Campbell and Los Gatos.

Since news was never plentiful on that beat, I started prowling around the mountains in search of feature material. I soon became involved in talking to the few remaining old-timers and their families, reading old diaries, and plowing through old county histories and other documents—in short, absorbing the true stories, tall tales, and lore of the region. Only later did I find that I had in fact gathered a great deal of basic historical source material.

By chance, I had stumbled into the end of an era in that part of the Santa Cruz Mountains, at the time of the transition from homesteads to weekend homes, from a rural economy to one based on highways, trucks, and autos. The changes then in progress were drastic, and permanent. Not one of the villages I wrote about in 1934 exists as such today, and all but one or two have vanished without a trace.

Some present-day readers may find the title of "Ghost Towns" misleading, considering the current popularity of books about mining camps and Gold Rush settlements. The communities described here were tiny hamlets, not towns, and none were mining camps. The image of ghost towns created by TV oat operas is one of places like Tombstone, Bodie, Calico, or any of the Mother Lode boom-and-bust towns, each with a dusty main street lined with saloons and bawdy houses, a boot hill filled with hundreds of graves, and a daily shoot-out with the sheriff looking on.

The Santa Cruz Mountain hamlets I wrote about forty-five years ago had none of these stock attributes. Only one, Wright's Station at the peak of construction on the narrow-gauge railroad, came close to the current TV image. All the others thrived briefly on lumbering, agriculture, the railroad, the highways, and then they all faded into total obscurity. They are memories, not ghosts. It is probably significant that no new, permanent communities have arisen in their place.

I have made relatively few changes in the original text of these stories save to omit and correct some glaring errors, rearrange some sections to make the narrative flow more easily, eliminate a few extraneous and repetitive passages, and to add dates, (1934) (1979), where I have felt they were needed to clarify confusion between past and present.

I have also inserted some current "author's notes" to explain where so many of the places mentioned in the series have gone, since it is all but impossible to find any trace of most of them. Only Holy City, which was still thriving as a highway tourist trap in 1934, now has enough old buildings to look like a tiny ghost town. It is a village that has almost, but not quite, vanished like the rest.

Historical markers, not always accurately placed, purport to show where some places—such as Patchen—once stood. An old church still holds Sunday services at Skyland; a chicken ranch now surrounds the old schoolhouse at Burrell. The old Burrell telephone exchange, nerve center of the region for decades, and its neighboring blacksmith shop, have vanished, along with the Wright mansion and the Wright Presbyterian church that stood across the way.

Wright's Station, largest and liveliest of the old railroad towns, is not even shown on present-day road maps. Its site is marked only by the gaping mouth of the tunnel to Laurel and the rustic steel bridge across Los Gatos Creek. The town started to die when the railroad stopped running in 1940; the last of its tumbledown buildings were razed by the San Jose Water Company years ago as part of a watershed protection project.

Across Los Gatos Creek and higher up the mountainside, no trace remains of Austrian Gulch and Germantown, once-flourishing colonies that lie under the waters of Lake Elsman behind Austrian Dam. Another reservoir farther down the creek, close to Los Gatos, completely engulfs the sites of Lexington and Alma, behind Lexington Dam.

At Glenwood, a historical marker commemorates the location of a busy village deserted first by the railroad and then by the main highway. The name is preserved in roads like Glenwood Drive leading in from Scotts Valley, Glenwood Cut-off leading down from Highway 17 (the freeway), and portions of the old Glenwood Highway still in use. But even former residents of the town have a hard time locating the site of the big hotel and the railroad station, and the railroad tunnel mouth is completely obscured by a tangle of brush, vines, and second-growth timber.

Other roads mentioned in the original "Ghost Towns" series are still on the map and in use. Summit Road, now paved and realigned, is a popular extension of the Skyline Boulevard, branching at Burrell to become Loma Prieta Avenue and the San Jose-Soquel Road.

The road up Loma Prieta, after leaving a cluster of weekend homes near Burrell, is not for the timid, and is all but impassable in wet weather. Its upper end is closed to protect the elaborate electronic installations that sprout from its summit and all along the ridge to Mt. Umunhum to the north and Mt. Madonna to the south. Highland Way still runs on down from the Soquel Road at Hall's Bridge (now a culvert) to join Eureka Canyon Road leading to Corralitos. It is paved and usually passable but subject to slides.

All in all, any effort to seek out the sites of most of the communities described in the stories must prove futile except for the most diligent of perusers of topographic maps and perhaps for the very few remaining old inhabitants who can remember the region's days of glory.

—John V. Young, 1979

Preface to the 2002 Edition
By Molly Young Brown

My copy of the first hardback edition of Ghost Towns has an inscription from my father, John Young: "Don't wait 45 years to publish your first book. Popsy" The 45 years referred to the time between his initial newspaper series and the book publication. My dad was 70 years old when Ghost Towns was first published, having written travel articles for the New York Times and other publications since his mid-fifties. He went on to write and publish five more books over the next 12 years. He was engaged in writing a sixth when he decided he was putting himself under too much pressure for a man his age, and "retired." He continued writing for some years after, however, mostly working on his memoirs, which he titled "My Life and What Of It?" and sent out a chapter at a time to a privileged circle of family and friends.

John Young died in 1999 at the age of 90. His wife, children, grandchildren, and great grandchildren are very pleased to have this new edition of his first book made available. The history of his beloved Santa Cruz Mountains will continue to fascinate old-timers and newcomers to this part of the world, a portion of which is now known as Silicon Valley. Mountain Charley, O. B. Castle, and the long-gone denizens of Patchen could never have imagined in their wildest dreams what would become of their rough-and-tumble frontier land, nor did John when he first wrote about its history in 1934, nor even in 1979 when the book was first published. As he neared the end of his life, John continued in dreams to roam this land of his youth and young adulthood, remembering it as it was many years ago.

Introduction

"The adjacent mountains were wild and rugged, the canyons deep and dark with the shadows of the forest. Coyotes broke the stillness with their dismal howls, and herds of deer slaked their thirst in the clear waters of the San Lorenzo river. Grizzly bears were numerous, prowling about in herds like hogs on a farm."

Comparing this early description of the Santa Cruz Mountains, written by some forgotten padre before the founding of the Spanish missions, with present-day scenes in one of California's growing playlands, it is difficult for city dwellers to comprehend the romantic and tradition-filled background of this region.

Equally difficult to understand at first glance when viewing the fertile Santa Clara Valley is why the first American settlers and the hordes of ranchers that followed the Gold Rush turned to the mountains for their homesteads. Homes were hewed from the tangled forest and even more tangled chaparral of the hillsides while vast level acres lay untouched below. But there was a reason—a good one at the time. By the time the Yankee settlers and their families had started to arrive in numbers, early in the 1850s, all the land in the Valley had been taken up, and an amazing conflict of titles jammed the courts with litigation for another half a century.

Mexican grants, a few Spanish grants, church and pueblo titles, and other claims rendered uncertain the most expansive of holdings as well as the smallest. No man knew whether the land he settled upon was to be his or his neighbor's tomorrow. Deeds were often obscurely worded and boundaries depended on haphazard surveys using trees, rocks, and stream beds as reference points. Distances were measured on horseback or by guesswork.

The native Indians had long ceased to be a problem, having dwindled from an estimated tens of thousands before the arrival of the

Spanish to mere handfuls after the Gold Rush. They were believed to have migrated from the upper Sacramento Valley, where the evidence of burial grounds (not found in the Santa Cruz Mountains) indicated they had lived for several thousand years.

Grizzly bears also were on the decline, far fewer than the "prowling herds" of Spanish times, although instances of their depredations were noted from time to time. Cougars and wildcats were the chief menace to livestock.

The mountains remained unexplored, to all intents and purposes, until the coming of the Yankee settlers, except for a few old trails used by hunters and trappers, and the old Spanish mission trail that connected Santa Cruz and San Jose.

Nearly two hundred years before the founding of the missions in the late 1770s, the Spanish explorer Sebastián Vizcáino, on a visit to Monterey Bay (which he named) in 1602, had noted the abundance of game in the foothills. Father Crespi scouted the Soquel region in 1769, when Portolá's expedition sought in vain for Monterey Bay, which lay just over the hills almost at their feet.

A military expedition led by Diego de Borica, Spanish commander of California, from Santa Cruz to Santa Clara in 1796, gave no description of the country. Don Miguel Riviera, Spanish military leader, set out from Santa Cruz early in 1790 to explore the southwest mountain region, and was said to have planted a cross on the site of a proposed outpost, but the plan was dropped. The journal of Colonel James Olyman, an American frontiersman who followed the same trail in 1845, is equally barren of detail.

It remained for Captain John C. Frémont, the famous "Pathfinder" of California history, to provide a more or less complete description of the topography, climate, and forest cover, in his memoirs of his trip from Los Gatos to Monterey in February, 1846. (Author's note—A plaque in Henry Cowell Redwoods State Park in Felton now commemorates Frémont's visit.)

To this unknown land came the intrepid homesteaders of the 1850s. It was a land of amazing timber, of plentiful water and grass, of mineral and forest wealth from which sprang many and varied industries. Mining for everything from lead to gold, primitive logging, milling, tanning, and hunting provided a full livelihood for the industrious.

One necessity peculiar to the valley farms added materially to the early development of forest resources of the mountains—fences. In those days it was up to each rancher to keep roaming cattle, horses and sheep out, not up to the owner of the animals to keep them in, and barbed wire was not to be invented for another quarter-century. Thus with the growth of large ranches came an enormous demand for fences, pickets, posts, and rails, and for grape stakes and other split lumber for which redwood was admirably suited. Not only did it split easily, but it was rot-resistant beyond belief.

Starting with split lumber and tanbark, a booming mountain industry sprang up in the first decade after the coming of the settlers, changing the tangled wilderness into one of the state's busiest regions almost overnight, or so it seemed.

Skid roads and ox trails interlaced the hills, and the vast wealth of the redwoods began to pour out in an ever-growing stream through what were to become Los Gatos and Saratoga, and into Santa Cruz. Sawmills, paper mills, tanneries, flour mills, and factories of every description lined the lower reaches of all the principal streams. Crude slab-sided homes with dirt floors occupied the open swales and hastily cleared land. Every usable stream was followed to its source as the urgent demand for water grew—water for power, water for logging flumes, water for irrigation, and water for domestic use.

The opening of the narrow-gauge railroad through the mountains from Los Gatos to Santa Cruz in 1880 was the most important event in Santa Cruz Mountain history since the arrival of the first white settlers. It wiped out towns that had existed for years; it brought new communities into being overnight; and it changed the face of the land. Nothing was ever quite the same again after the railroad.

Wagon roads followed the railroad, highways followed the roads, and automobiles and trucks eventually arrived on the scene to rob the railroad of its once-unchallenged role in the economics of the region. Today (1934) new highways are leaving stranded towns that have thrived for scores of years, and shortly they will cause the establishment of new communities. No railroad station is now open between Los

Gatos and Felton, although heavier rails are being laid in anticipation of increased summer traffic. Summer cottages and permanent residences had started to flourish in the mountains before the Great Depression, and are increasing again in some of the larger tracts, a far cry from the pioneer cabins of the 1850s.

The day of the mountain family, of plain, homespun "mountain folks," has passed; a new era is in the making, burying in the annals of long ago the last traces of a colorful and romantic past.

Mountain Charley

Most colorful of Santa Cruz Mountain characters of the pioneer days was Mountain Charley McKiernan, one of the first white settlers in the region. Hunter, rancher, teamster, road-builder and stage-line operator, McKiernan was said to be the idol of every small boy who grew up in the region. According to his admirers, his motto was: "Right wrongs nobody."

The simple statement, "I knew Mountain Charley," was the proud boast of many an old mountain man, and tales of this half-legendary figure have long survived him. After he was disfigured by a bear in a fight that is a legend in itself, it was said of McKiernan that no grizzly would argue with him over the right-of-way on a trail, a typical tall tale that in no way detracted from McKiernan's sterling reputation.

Charles Henry McKiernan was born in Ireland in 1825 (or possibly 1830). As a young quartermaster in the British army, he traveled to Australia and New Zealand, where he was stationed when word came of the California gold strike of 1848. His enlistment having expired, he signed on as a seaman on a ship headed for San Francisco. Not waiting for their pay, the crew members jumped ship to join recruiters who met them at the pier with bottles of whiskey as inducements to work in the mines. The wages were up to $20 a day. In Ireland at the time of McKiernan's departure the prevailing scale was about $20 a year.

With his savings from his first year's work in the mines McKiernan organized a pack train to carry supplies to the Trinity mining district of northern California. Attacked by Indians on his second trip, McKiernan and his company lost everything but their lives.

Back at the mines, McKiernan accumulated a second stake and headed out for the Santa Clara Valley. There he found that conflicting claims to all the land made investment quite inadvisable. With a friend named Page, he entered the Santa Cruz Mountains early in 1850 to look for available land to homestead.

This cabin, built by McKiernan's nephew, is close to the site of the Mountain Charley homestead.

Following an old Indian trail from what is now Los Gatos, the two men stopped at a small pond the Spanish padres had called *Laguna del Sargento, a* long-time favorite camping place of the Indians. On the site were quantities of mortars, pestles, and flint arrowheads. Page went on to Santa Cruz, but McKiernan found the spot to his liking, and there he settled, completely alone. He established his homestead on the highest point of the ridge, where the southwest corner of Redwood Estates now joins Summit Road.

Near a spring McKiernan later built a frame house, said to have been the first such structure in the entire mountain range, from redwood lumber whipsawed on the spot. (Whip-sawing was a crude form of lumbering performed by two men using a long, thin, flexible sawblade with handles at both ends. One man stood in a pit under the log, the other man on top, alternately pulling up and down on the saw to make the cut. It was brutal work, but it did the job. Lumber cut in this fashion was worth about $100 a thousand board feet in those days).

His home and corrals completed, McKiernan started to raise sheep and cattle and to hunt deer for market; but grizzly bears, cougars and wildcats soon made mincemeat of the sheep. Long-horned steers, better able to cope with the predators, were sold for $6 to $8 a head, mainly for their hides and tallow.

Deer meat was worth 10¢ a pound and was easy to obtain, at first. Since the deer had never heard the sound of a rifle before, they were still feeding by day and would only look around in curiosity when one of their number fell to McKiernan's muzzle-loading blunderbuss.

McKiernan made two trips a week to Alviso (in those days a seaport on south San Francisco Bay) with deer meat to be shipped to San Francisco. He was alone in the mountains until 1853, when the Lyman John Burrell family settled farther down the ridge, above the site where the town of Wright's later located. In the same year, one John Bean settled on Bean Creek near the present town of Glenwood, and Charles C. Martin homesteaded land adjoining McKiernan's. Martin operated a stage line and toll road on the Mountain Charley road, and later built a home in the Valley for his family.

There were no roads west of San Jose at that time, and no fences. Until McKiernan and his neighbors hacked out an ox-trail, later to become a stage route, only an Indian trail crossed the Santa Cruz Mountains. McKiernan later built several roads, one of which still bears his name. It was a cut-off route out of Los Gatos, running up through Moody Gulch near what is now Holy City, and across the site of Redwood Estates to join the old Indian trail near McKiernan's home.

(Author's note—Portions of this road are still in use, mainly by local residents, running south from Summit Road near its junction with Highway 17 to join the old Glenwood Highway at Scotts Valley. It is narrow and winding, having only one lane with turnouts. The site of his cabin is designated by a historical marker.)

McKiernan, along with many others, tried his hand at gold mining on and near his property, even to the extent of staking out a claim in company with four other men, but nothing came of the venture. No paying amounts of gold were ever found in these mountains.

The Famous Bear Fight

Even for a region as rich in legendary lore as the Santa Cruz Mountains, the story of Mountain Charley McKiernan's fight with a grizzly bear is outstanding as a tale of heroism and fortitude, one that has needed no embellishment (although many versions exist). As told (1934) by McKiernan's son, James, residing at the old home place near the summit, the legend differs only in minor detail from several other versions current at the time.

Grizzly bears in the 1850s were too plentiful for the ranchers, who hunted them relentlessly to stop depredations on their livestock. They also made a profit selling bear hides and meat. The grizzlies were huge, shaggy creatures weighing from 800 to 1,200 pounds (the only species of bear in these mountains), and were always treated with respect. They were best hunted from an uphill stand with a fast horse ready for a quick getaway if necessary. Often it took several bullets to put a grizzly out of action. McKiernan had often shot grizzly bears; in fact, he was one of the best known bear hunters in the mountains.

On May 8, 1854, McKiernan and a friend named Taylor started out for a gulch about a mile southwest of the McKiernan place, where Taylor was planning to take up some land. After shooting a couple of deer, the two men spotted a she-grizzly with two cubs. As both men were excellent shots, they decided to go for the bear and headed up the gulch to approach the animal from above.

When they arrived at their chosen spot, the bear and her cubs had disappeared. Following a deer trail in pursuit, they came upon the she-bear around a bend, standing and facing McKiernan at a distance of no more than six feet, her forepaws outstretched for a raking hug.

McKiernan fired instantly, with the muzzle of his gun up against the bear's chest, while Taylor fired over McKiernan's head into the bear's face. McKiernan reversed his gun to club the bear with the stock, but the bear beat down the weapon and seized him with her powerful forepaws, crushed the front of his skull in her jaws, then tossed him aside and started for Taylor.

Meanwhile Taylor's small dog had attacked the two cubs. Their squalling distracted the mother and she turned to their rescue, giving Taylor a chance to escape to the ridge top, supposing that McKiernan had been killed instantly. The bear chased the dog away, then returned to McKiernan and dragged him to the end of a clearing under an oak tree and after pawing him over left him. The bear was never seen again.

His rifle reloaded, Taylor returned to the scene to find McKiernan sitting up and conscious, but paralyzed from the waist down. The fight had lasted only seconds, and McKiernan said he had been fully conscious all the time and had recalled every act of his life in the process.

Taylor bound up McKiernan's head with his shirt and leaving his loaded rifle for protection went for help. Accounts differ as to whether a doctor came to the ranch to attend McKiernan, or whether he was taken either to San Jose or to Santa Cruz for the medical attention.

In any case, the doctor hammered a silver plate out of two Mexican dollars and fitted it into the broken place in McKiernan's skull where the bear had chewed away the bone over his left eye up to the top of the frontal bone. Within three weeks the plate had started to corrode and had to be removed, to be replaced some time later with another plate. McKiernan suffered through the entire ordeal without anesthetics until the wound healed. He suffered from severe headaches for two years, however, until a specialist in Redwood City removed the second plate and found a lock of hair under it. By this time anesthesia had become more generally available, sparing McKiernan the pain of the third operation.

Although terribly disfigured (he wore a hat low over his left eye the rest of his life), McKiernan enjoyed full health until 1890, when he became ill with an obscure stomach ailment. He died on January 18, 1892, thirty-eight years after the bear fight that made him famous.

The Mountain Charley Big Tree

One of the lesser-known landmarks of the region is the "Mountain Charley Big Tree," named for McKiernan after loggers had ceased operations in the area.

A coastal redwood (*Sequoia sempervirens*) originally estimated to have been 300 feet high, the tree today (1934) stands 260 feet at its tip, which was broken off in a storm long ago. It is situated on private property 300 feet from the old Santa Cruz Highway at Big Redwood Park, a subdivision half a mile north of Glenwood.

One of the largest trees left in the Santa Cruz Mountains, it is 20 feet in diameter at its base, 63 feet in circumference, and an estimated five feet in diameter at its top. It was apparently spared because it was too big to handle in the rather inaccessible gulch where it stands. (Author's note—The tree still stands but is difficult to see from the road.)

Mt. Charley Big Tree, c. 1969.

More Bear Fights

Mountain Charley McKiernan was not the only well-known mountain man to be attacked by a bear, although he was more fortunate, or harder to kill, than most other victims. Many a disappearance was blamed on bears or bandits, a convenient method of getting rid of enemies perhaps.

Probably the last recorded and authentic incidence of a bear attack was the one that proved fatal in 1875 for William H. Waddell, a pioneer lumberman and former owner of the Theodore Hoover Rancho del Oso (Bear) on Waddell Creek. Waddell was hunting on his ranch when he was attacked by a grizzly bear which his dogs had cornered. He was so severely bitten he died five days after being rescued from the bear by a companion.

The last grizzly bear of record in the Santa Cruz Mountains was killed on Ben Lomond Mountain in November, 1886, according to Leon Rowland, Santa Cruz County historian.

Over on the other side of the mountain at Lexington, then known as Jones' Mill, a lurid tale is told of a bear fight that makes up in persistence what it may lack in accuracy, for it is told from one end of the range to the other whenever bear fights are mentioned in saloons.

The hero of the tale was a gigantic Frenchman whose name has been lost. He was built on the general lines of a Primo Camera, with a mighty barrel chest, enormous biceps and ham-like fists. He feared neither God nor man, and had a particular dislike for grizzly bears.

On this occasion (probably in the 1850s), he was hunting in a glen above the mill when he suddenly encountered a full-grown grizzly, which immediately charged. The Frenchman attempted to hold her off with his gun, but the bear knocked it aside and grabbed him in her front paws.

In desperation the Frenchman thrust his left wrist between the bear's jaws and with his right fist proceeded to slug the bear on its unprotected front quarters. Back and forth they wrestled, man and bear, while the Frenchman's arm was reduced to hamburger; but, it is recorded, the bear was first to quit. She unlimbered her jaws, ducked a parting swipe from the Frenchman's mighty fist, and lit out for the tall timber.

Friends of the Frenchman found him unconscious, his left arm hanging in shreds. With the rude surgery of the time, they cut off what was left of the arm, cauterized the stump, and in due course the Frenchman returned to work.

The bear? Well, as the story goes, they found her the next day, lying dead in a gulch, her insides pounded to a pulp from the Frenchman's terrible blows. Less spectacular but probably more authentic is the story told by Frank Howell, son of the founder of Reservoir Ranch two miles above Lexington. Howell's father discovered one morning that a horse on his ranch which had died of eating some poisonous weed had become a feast for a bear. Howell and young Alex Ogan, a relative, moved the carcass underneath a nearby tree and over it built a platform twenty feet off the ground, knowing that grizzly bears do not or cannot climb trees.

Just after moon-rise that night the bear, a large female with cubs, returned. Both men fired from their perch, wounding the mother. She squalled, rolled over, and staggered back into the brush. Howell fired again and wounded one of the cubs. At this point Howell's two large dogs, liberated by Mrs. Howell when she heard the shots, charged into the scene. The dogs jumped the cub and eventually killed it.

Knowing the ways of wounded grizzlies, the two men stayed on their perch until daylight. When they ventured down, they found no sign of the mother bear but did see buzzards circling over the woods a mile or so away.

Later, in 1866, Howell and young Ogan went out to look for a missing cow and found her dead. She had been partly eaten, apparently by a bear. Evidently the cow, running away from the bear in panic, had run into a tree and broken her neck. As the bear signs around the carcass were fresh, the two men did not linger on the scene. It was one of the last bears ever seen on the eastern side of the ridge.

The Summit District

The tops of the mountains, with their park-like natural clearings, their fine stands of timber, and their lagoons, attracted settlers as did no other part of the mountain region.

Hence it was by a lagoon at the present-day intersection of the old Los Gatos-Santa Cruz Highway with Summit Road that John Martin Schultheis and his wife, the former Susan Byerly, took up a homestead early in 1852 and erected a home of split lumber that stands today as sound as it was eighty-two years ago. (Author's note—Believed to be the oldest building in the Santa Cruz Mountains, the house is at the rear of 22849 Summit Road. It has, however, been covered with new lumber.)

A German cabinetmaker by trade, Schultheis was a skilled craftsman, able to transform his crude materials into finished lumber so smooth it defies the eye to detect it from the factory-made lumber that now covers its exterior. Mortar, made of lime packed on mule-back from the quarries near present-day Felton, was used to chink up the square log walls to cement together the homemade bricks for the chimney.

The lagoon, from which the family obtained their water for many years, became known as Schultheis Lagoon, which is how it appears on maps published in later years. The little pond, framed by redwoods and surrounded by a split-rail fence, eventually dried up and was unknown for many years. During the past two or three years, however, heavy rains have revived its springs and a considerable expanse of water was visible this past spring (1934).

After the Civil War, in 1869, a Union soldier named Volney Averill wandered into the Santa Cruz Mountains. He left, but returned in 1873 to stay, for he had met Alice Schultheis, daughter of John and Susan. They were married June 2, 1873, on the old ranch.

The following year Averill bought fifteen acres of land he cleared for an orchard, later adding more land until he had seventy-five acres under cultivation, including thirty-five acres in prunes. Their ranch straddled the Santa Clara-Santa Cruz County line just outside the huge old Spanish land grant called Rancho Soquel Augmentation. (Author's note—Averill's son Arthur and his wife were running the ranch at the time this article was written and provided much of this material.)

The Chases

Next-door neighbors of the Schultheis and Averill families were the Chases, who arrived in the early 1860s. Foster Chase came in 1867 to join his brother Joseph (Josiah) who had established a saw-mill near Hall's Bridge on the Soquel River. Foster owned a ranch just south of the Averill place.

In the spring of 1868 Foster took charge of his brother's lumber mill at Lexington and continued in this job until 1873, when the plant was moved back to the Summit district. He remained in charge there until the plant was closed in the 1880s. Foster then took over his brother's ranch and managed it until he was able to buy the place in 1890, making many improvements. He then owned 180 acres along Soquel Road.

In 1870 Foster married Nancy Howell at Lexington. She was the daughter of a Valley pioneer, Watkins F. Howell, who had earlier settled on what was to become Reservoir Ranch in 1856. The San Jose Water Company's Howell Reservoir above Lexington was named for him. Chase was very active in the affairs of the little community that had grown up around the lagoon, and for several years he served as a trustee for the Summit school at its several locations.

A portion of the original home of Joseph W. Chase, built in the late 1850s by a man named Taylor, is still standing (1934) with additions and improvements made by Chase when he bought it in 1862. It is occupied by Ralph and Maude Chase, son and daughter of Chase.

Well known in the Summit district was another Taylor family, "Uncle Jimmy," and "Aunt Margaret" Taylor, who attended all the weddings and funerals in the region for nearly forty years. Kindly and benevolent, they were loved throughout the mountains. Their home was off Soquel Road south of the Chase residence.

James "Uncle Jimmy" Taylor came to the mountains in 1857, moving several times before finally settling down in 1864. He had married "Aunt Margaret" Higgins several years before. They had no children of their own, but adopted William Dennis, son of William and Ann Tillman Dennis, early settlers in the region. The boy's mother had died in childbirth, and the Taylors gave him a home and raised him to manhood.

William Dennis Taylor, as he became known, grew up to become a popular and prosperous rancher and served as clerk and trustee of Summit school for years before he died in 1919. His foster parents had died earlier—"Uncle Jimmy" in 1899, "Aunt Margaret" in 1898 when she was past ninety years of age.

Between the Taylor and Chase ranches the famous Summit Hotel was established in 1887. A small hostelry operated by Fred Loomis, it flourished for years as a summer resort, supplied with clientele mostly by stage from Wright's Station on the narrow-gauge railroad. The hotel was taken over in the 1890s by A. N. Nichols, and it was maintained by him and others until 1910 when it was converted into a private residence.

On the other side of the road was Rasmus Neilson's blacksmith shop. Neilson, a widower, went east in 1888 to marry a second time, according to E. E. Place of Los Gatos. While he was away, his eighteen-year-old son, George, was accidentally killed in a hunting accident, providing a tragic homecoming for his father.

Other early settlers in the Summit district were Moses M. Hanger, who settled on the south side of the road near the lagoon in the 1870s, and Judge W. H. Aitken of San Francisco, who retired there in the 1880s.

In 1899 the cornerstone was laid for a branch of the Los Gatos Christ Episcopal Church. The building became a fine example of miniature Gothic architecture when it was completed within the year with the aid of public subscriptions. Pastors from Los Gatos and other towns held services there regularly for many years, until a population decline after World War I finally led to its abandonment. Hidden in a dense grove of second-growth redwoods and oaks atop a little knoll across Summit Road from Schultheis lagoon, the church was within a stone's throw of the old Los Gatos-Santa Cruz Highway but remained unsuspected by passing thousands of motorists.

Vandals, however, had long since discovered the beautiful little church and had stripped out most of the interior woodwork, defaced the marble altar, and marred the walls. Tramps used it for a lodging place from time to time. (Author's note—The church burned to the ground some time before 1940.)

The Santa Cruz Turnpike

Not far from the old church is a clearing on the Averill ranch where one of the first stage depots in the Santa Cruz Mountains was situated in a large barn, which burned down half a century ago. The barn served the stage run which was started in 1863 by the Santa Cruz Gap Turnpike Joint Stock Company, which had been granted franchises by the supervisors of the two counties.

Running up the west side of Los Gatos Canyon and replacing the old Jones Hill stage road, the San Jose Turnpike (as it came to be known) joined at Woodwardia the route of the older stage line which had been established in 1856–58 by F. A. Hihn and associates. Built by the Hihn Company as a competitive route to the Mountain Charley stage line, it followed approximately the same route as the present Soquel Road, which has recently (1934) been widened and straightened for modern automobile use.

Originally called the Morrell cut-off, the Turnpike turned west from the Morrell homestead, through which it once passed, and emerged at the Sears ranch. In the 1860s Smith and George Comstock, who were cutting timber on the McMillan (Young) holdings, found the grade too steep and made a new road across the back country to the Chase mill at Hall's Bridge. This route later joined the main road past the Morrell place and connected with Burrell and Wright's. Hiram Morrell built the section now in use to eliminate the ruinous dust,

Patchen Episcopal Church, c. 1934. It no longer exists.

which spoiled his grape crops, from the traffic in teams and stages through what had once been his front yard.

New Word About an Old-Timer

A letter received by the *San Jose Mercury Herald* on July 22, 1934, offers added information about an early settler in the Summit region, the great-grandfather of Miss Frances Rupp of Dos Palos. Miss Rupp writes:

"Jonathan Augustus Dryden, better known as Gus Dryden, with his wife and six children, crossed the plains in a covered wagon in 1861, and after two years in San Jose settled in the Santa Cruz Mountains. At that time Henry Dryden (Miss Rupp's grandfather) was six years old.

"Shortly later the building of the Summit school was begun and Gus Dryden helped to build it. He was one of the trustees all the time he was there. After seven years at Summit he moved his family to Paicines.

"Henry Dryden received his first schooling at the Summit school, where he went with the children of John Martin Schultheis and those of Mountain Charley McKiernan.

"Gus Dryden bought the old Gommer place, situated half a mile above where Holy City is now. Where he used to have his hay fields and a cow pasture, a modern resort (Redwood Estates) now stands. He also tended the toll gate at his place (at the junction of the Santa Cruz Gap Turnpike with the Mountain Charley road).

"The stump on which the bear now stands (at the entrance to Redwood Estates) was then used as a playhouse by the Dryden children. The old Dutch windmill is where the public watering trough for teams formerly was."

Perambulating Patchen

The perambulating post office for the Summit region for more than half a century was Patchen (or Patchin), which had at least half a dozen locations up and down Summit road from 1872 until 1925. The story of its name is one of the more amusing semi- legends of the area.

Because it was first situated on the Fowler ranch, at the junction of Mountain Charley Road and the old Santa Cruz Highway, it was assumed by the local residents that the new post office would be called Fowler's Station, or Fowler's Summit, according to the custom of the time. But the postal inspector who was assigned the duty of formally establishing the post office and giving it a name did not like that selection, for some unknown reason. Perhaps there was already a post office named Fowler's elsewhere in the state.

As the story goes, the inspector stepped out of the stagecoach in front of Fowler's place to encounter an old man sitting on the doorstep busily sewing.

"What are you doing?" asked the inspector, seeking to establish friendly relations with the natives.

"Patchin'," replied the old man, and that was that.

In any event, the post office name was confirmed and appears on the government record as having been established at Patchen (not Patchin) on March 28, 1872. (Local history is a little confusing on this point, since the house in which Fowler handled the mail was not built until 1876).

Local residents for years insisted that the spelling was wrong, as well as the origin of the name. They claimed the post office was named after a famous race horse with the improbable handle of George M. Patchen. The authoritative volume, *California Place Names*, published in 1925, gives the name as Patchin, but states that it was named for the racehorse. Many a heated argument arose over that point at meetings

1866 view of Patchen, looking south.

of the Santa Cruz Mountain Social and Improvement Club, successor to the once-flourishing Floral Society.

One long-time resident, Charles W. C. Murdock of Alma, the stepson of Louis Hebard, remembers his mother's telling of how the place was named. According to her, great discussion arose over the naming of the post office. When the postal inspector arrived, the name was still up in the air.

To settle the argument, Mrs. Hebard suggested asking the first man who came up the road to provide a name—that man was William "Billy" Brown, well known in the region.

"Why," quoth Bill, "call it Patchen," referring to the race horse. And Patchen it was.

Murdock also recalls that the mail, previous to the establishment of the post office, had been deposited in a hollow tree nearby, and the customers all sorted their own mail.

Josiah Fowler was the son of Jacob Fowler, who bought 240 acres of land to establish a ranch and sold it to his son before he died in 1875. The son cleared forty acres for fruit, but sold thirty acres of it. In 1882 he married Abbie A. Proseus and two years later built a larger house, now known as the Laddick place, in the same location. Widely known in the mountains, Fowler served for years as roadmaster for Lexington and Wright's precincts.

Meanwhile, the post office called Patchen did not stay put, but went bounding around the landscape, following each newly appointed postmaster to his home. The next place after Fowler's was at the home of D. C. Feely, who gained brief fame at the time of his death by having bequeathed his entire fortune of $40,000 to the Socialist party. His place was about half a mile north of Fowler's, on the present-day Harry Ryan ranch.

Next stop was half a mile south of Fowler's station, where Joshua White presided over a ranch known as the White & Gibson place. From there the post office went to a popular summer resort known as Edgemont, run by Mr. and Mrs. L. N. Scott, in 1882. Scott died in 1907, but the resort was still in operation in 1934. The post office, however, had been discontinued in 1925 (as it turned out, only temporarily).

In addition to its postal duties, Patchen was headquarters for the Patchen Social Club, which later became the Santa Cruz Mountain Improvement Club, combining with a former literary society. (Author's note—In 1934 the original charter still had two years to run, although by then it had long been almost forgotten.) There was an opera house as well. Before the turn of the century, a stock company headed by Volney Averill, with Charles Aitken as secretary, was formed with the intention of building a community hall. This was soon accomplished, and the finished product was promptly dubbed "Summit Opera House." Shakespearean drama coached by Charles Wilkinson, an Englishman and former actor, also entertained the community. Traveling road companies played there often, and many neighborhood socials and musical parties used its facilities.

(Author's note—The building remained in use until the early 1940s, when it was torn down and the lumber hauled to Laurel for another building, according to *Historic Spots in California.*)

The Rise and Fall of Holy City (1979)

Holy City, on the old Santa Cruz Highway a little north of the Summit, was a Johnny-come-lately to the ranks of ghost towns of the Santa Cruz Mountains, and is the only one that still looks like a movie version of a ghost town, lacking only tumbleweeds and a deserted saloon. Saloons it never had.

Here the perambulating post office of Patchen came to rest under a new name—after being resurrected in 1927. The town was flourishing when the "Ghost Towns" series was published, but died a few years later when another highway realignment left it high and dry.

Holy City was founded in 1918 by William E. "Father" Riker, a persistent candidate for governor, who advocated, among other things, white supremacy, communal living, and total abstinence. He gathered about him a small colony of followers, mostly elderly, who shared his views and were willing to share their meager savings as well.

Soon a gaggle of flimsy wooden structures embellished with garish signs sprang up on both sides of the highway to lure passing tourists to buy gasoline, food, souvenirs and the like. It was a welcome resting

Billboards for Holy City. The letters P.C.D.W. Stand for "Perfect Christian Divine Way."

Telescopes at the Holy City observatory.

Dancing, dining, and movies were among the attractions
at Holy City.

place for motorists with boiling radiators stuck in the bumper-to-bumper traffic that often jammed the highway on a weekend.

Proclaiming that it was "headquarters for the world's most perfect government" (namely, Father Riker in person), Holy City soon acquired a weekly newspaper, a radio station, a restaurant, a service station, and rest rooms. Riker also ran a mineral water business on the side.

But when Highway 17 by-passed Holy City in 1940, it declined rapidly. A few tumbledown buildings on one side of the old highway face the still-active post office in an abandoned store on the other side, but that is all that remains of the once-thriving highway stop today.

According to *Historic Spots in California,* Riker stayed on into the 1960s and surprised everyone by joining the Catholic church at the age of 93.

The Railroad

Where wagons by the score, bearing produce of every description, once lined up to load long freight trains at several railroad stations in the Santa Cruz Mountains, today not a depot is open on the line between Los Gatos and Felton.

Though in its decline it may well be, the railroad has played a part of immeasurable economic importance not only in the speed and the magnitude of development of the region, but in the direction of that development as well.

The railroad originally was proposed to run through the mountains not by way of present-day Los Gatos but through Saratoga (then called McCartysville) and over the Summit in the vicinity of Waterman's Gap (at the present junction of State Highway 9 and the Big Basin road). It was to continue on down along the San Lorenzo River through Boulder Creek and connect with the Santa Cruz & Felton line at Felton.

Had this plan been followed, the difference would have been remarkable. For instance, Saratoga rather than Los Gatos would have become of major importance in the foothill region. Other towns that owed their existence and livelihood to the railroad—such as Alma, Wright's, Laurel, and Glenwood—might never have come into being.

Surveys, however, showed the Saratoga route to be impractical, or less practical, than the Los Gatos route despite all of its tunnels. Opposition from farmers in the San Tomas region, which the Saratoga route would have crossed, clinched the decision. The donation of a right-of-way through Los Gatos by J. W. Farwell, and in Aldercroft Gulch by the McMurtry family and others, also helped the decision.

The railroad was incorporated March 29, 1876, as the South Pacific Coast Railroad Company, under the leadership of James G. Fair, Alfred E. Davis, and associates. The line was headed from Alameda on the east side of the San Francisco Bay to Santa Cruz via Newark with the avowed intention of continuing down the Salinas Valley and over the Coast range to the San Joaquin Valley. Ultimately it was supposed to meet the Denver & Rio Grande narrow-gauge line then reaching for the coast, but the South Pacific never got past Felton, near Santa Cruz, where it linked up with the Felton & Santa Cruz line. This narrow-gauge railroad, built to connect with logging trains from Boulder Creek and the upper San Lorenzo River, had been completed in 1875.

Rail and ferry service was inaugurated on the South Pacific line on June 1, 1878, when a wharf was completed at Alameda Point. At first the service went only as far as Newark, twenty-five miles to the south. The remainder of the line took two years to construct.

Employing large gangs of Chinese laborers, the railroad builders followed a route up Los Gatos canyon past Lexington, an old stage coach station which it left high and dry on the wrong side of the canyon. The line then passed through Alma, another stage stop, which promptly assumed Lexington's former glory and most of its occupants. It next turned up Aldercroft Gulch to come to a halt at Wright's Station, known as "The Tunnel."

The tunnel itself, a mile and an eighth in length, was a nine-day's wonder in the mountains and brought the curious from miles around. During construction train passengers were taken from Wright's by stage over a temporary route to Felton. The tunnel was officially opened May 15, 1880, a historic occasion indeed for the mountain region. On account of the railroad work, great activity soon developed at Wright's and at the other end of the tunnel, where the tiny village of Laurel appeared overnight.

(Author's note—Laurel stood at the present junction of Laurel Road, Schultheis Road, and Redwood Lodge Road. The town's principal claim to fame was its location between Wright's Tunnel and Glenwood Tunnel. During construction of the railroad it was a supply depot and tie camp. Later it was headquarters for the Frederick Hihn lumber operations in that area, which according to the historical marker on the site provided much of the lumber for the reconstruction of San Francisco after the 1906 earthquake. There was a general store there run by the La Porte family, and a post office from 1882 to 1953. The boarded-up store is still standing. Just back from the road, the covered end of the Wright's tunnel is visible. Redwood Lodge Road used to run down to San Jose-Soquel Road but has now been rendered impassable by a wash-out.)

Tunneling in the Mountain

The tunnel itself, however, got off to a bad start, taking an undetermined number of Chinese lives in a disaster that has grown to enormous proportions in the telling over the decades.

Crude pine torches were carried by the "coolies" for illumination after the digging had progressed a short distance into the mountain. Nothing happened for a while, then one day a lusty blow from a pick opened up a pocket of natural gas.

The blast that resulted threw Chinese workers around like tenpins, blowing several out of the mouth of the shaft. The number of dead totaled 17, or 25, or 34, or 200, according to whose account you accept. In those days the Chinese were not reckoned in the same light as white men and were not accorded the dignity of so much as a coroner's inquest, let alone a formal count.

Some accounts from the time say the bodies of the Chinese were shipped back to China. Others claim their bones still lie in a ditch dug beside the tracks just outside the portal, and that their ghosts still haunt the lonely canyons around the tunnel.

The Earthquake and the Railroad

April 18, 1906, meant quite as much to the railroad and to the region it served as it did to San Francisco, the city that gave the great earthquake of that day its name.

Lying directly along the San Andreas fault line in some sections and across it in others, the railroad suffered heavily from the temblor. The tunnel at Wright's cracked in the middle and settled several inches out of line. The tracks just outside the portal were twisted sideways into several S-curves. Less serious slides blocked the Glenwood tunnel also, while a huge earth slide dammed the creek at Eva station, creating a natural lake that blocked all travel on that part of the line for months.

Railroad officials took advantage of the tie-up to convert the entire narrow-gauge line to standard gauge, which meant the tunnels had to be widened. The long tunnel at Wright's was reopened in August, 1907, just a month after Conductor Thomas O'Neil and a venturesome crew brought the first train through the Glenwood tunnel on July 1, 1907. The lake at Eva remained, despite heavy blasting, until December.

That was not all, however. Re-routing the tracks around some short tunnels that were being abandoned, straightening curves, rebuilding trestles, and other chores kept the line closed to through traffic exactly three years, one month, and eleven days. Reopening of the line with a schedule of fourteen trains daily was celebrated in Los Gatos on May 29, 1909, a great day in the mountains.

Switching the Gauges

Broad gauge tracks had reached Los Gatos from Campbell in the late 1890s, and a group of large shippers including the Hume company, Bill Rankin, Hook & Malpus and others soon succeeded in persuading the Southern Pacific that increased revenues would result from the change to larger cars. Prior to the change, a six cents per ton transfer charge was paid by the shippers for moving freight from narrow-gauge to broad-gauge cars at Campbell. When the third rail was laid alongside the narrow-gauge tracks a strange variety of transportation came into use.

Both broad-gauge and narrow-gauge cars were pulled by the same engine, but, since the broad-gauge cars were wider, they extended over to one side, and their coupling bars also had to be extended to provide for the diagonal connection with their narrow-gauge brothers. At first only freight was carried on this hybrid arrangement, but passenger cars were added by 1900 and the new service was extended to Wright's Station in 1903–04. Institution of wider, heavier and more comfortable cars on the broad-gauge tracks gave a decided impetus to the already growing tourist traffic at Wright's and the development of Sunset Park. By 1905 the railroad was enjoying patronage never before dreamed of, and not since equaled.

Tunnel Troubles

It was in this period that trouble arose over Tunnel No. 1, which earlier had been known as Tunnel No. 2. After both these tunnels were eliminated, the Wright's tunnel became No. 1, and the Glenwood tunnel No. 2.

The original Tunnel No. 1 was a short bore through a rocky shoulder near the trestle between Los Gatos and Alma, but it made up in difficulty what it lacked in length. Against warnings by engineers of the San Jose Water Company, whose main flume rounded the same shoulder less than fifty feet above the railroad tunnel, the railroad had cut through the shoulder. The widening of the bore for the third rail added to the damage, and soon slides began to bring down the roof and the flume above it.

Not only was the water supply for the town of Los Gatos cut off from time to time but also the electric lights. (The drop from the upper canyon to Los Gatos gave the water supply enough of a head to generate about two hundred horsepower, a major part of the town's energy needs.) The power company, headed by J. W. Farwell at the time, vigorously protested the frequent interruptions in service, and began to send bins to the railroad for the cost of fuel for auxiliary power.

These bills went to the Southern Pacific main office through the office of the San Jose agent, Paul Shoup, later to become president of the company. Shoup conferred with Farwell and others and many a heated wrangle resulted before they agreed to blast out the tunnel and make it into an open cut. But that was not the end of their troubles at that spot. Removing the toe of the rock shoulder destroyed the natural foundation of the entire ledge, and the whole hill began to move down. The problem took years to solve.

Confronted with a similar situation at the north portal of the Wright's tunnel in 1893, when a huge rock slide virtually wiped out part of the tunnel, railroad engineers devised a unique machine for clearing the debris, and then concreted the end of the tunnel to prevent future slides.

When the Southern Pacific took over the South Pacific line in 1887, it ended a confusion of names under which it was constructed in various stages: Santa Cruz & Felton; Bay & Coast; Oakland Township, San Francisco and Colorado River (!); Felton & Pescadero; and the Almaden Branch Railroad, all in addition to the South Pacific Railroad Company under which it started.

"The Tunnel" Becomes Wright's Station

The early history of the place that was to become Wright's Station (which is sometimes spelled without the apostrophe), if it had any, has been lost in the obscurity that so often veils the overnight rise of a boom town.

When the railroad arrived at the northern portal of the tunnel site at Wright's early in 1877, the only building was a tumbledown woodcutter's shack. This deficiency was soon repaired as workmen's shanties, a large cook-house, and tool sheds sprang up in rapid succession.

It was about that time that O. B. Castle, foreman over the gangs of Chinese laborers, built his notorious saloon, and "The Tunnel," as the settlement was then known, was off to a flying start. The brief years of construction prior to the opening of the tunnel in 1880 brought wild scenes of revelry to the saloon, home of Castle's "Famous Discovery."

The "Discovery," a sure-fire cure for all human ailments from hangnails to hangovers, was blamed for much of the disturbance. The recipe called for diluting one gallon of mountain dew (raw whiskey) with four tablespoons of water, and downing it at one sitting.

Small wonder that, according to Herbert Martin, a native of these mountains, who visited the place as a boy, The Tunnel made San Francisco's ill-famed Barbary Coast "look like a Sunday School picnic" by comparison. Housewives made repeated forays à la Carrie Nation, armed with chairs and brooms, whenever the celebrations approached the riot level.

With the completion of the railroad and the departure of the construction crews, the scene changed. The Tunnel became Wright's Station (named for the pioneer Wright family), lost most of its wildness, and began its rapid development into one of the principal towns of the mountain region.

Wright's Station, c. 1900. These buildings have all vanished.

By 1882 the town consisted of a store, hotel, saloon, blacksmith shop, a post office (since 1879), and the railroad station, besides some shacks or cottages where the hired help lived. Judge S. P. Hall was postmaster and storekeeper. Charles Grant bought out Castle and improved the town's only hostelry. A man named Woodruff was the town blacksmith and a very busy man indeed.

Then one Fourth of July, in 1885, an overheated stove set fire to the hotel, and the whole town burned to the ground. This happened shortly after A. J. Rich, a capitalist, had acquired all the property in the village, and it was Rich who rebuilt it, this time on the east side of the bridge before the tunnel.

Ralph Thompson erected a store of sorts in a collection of sheds while carrying on business after the fire in a boxcar parked on a siding. He automatically became postmaster, a job that went with the store. Ed Cottle ran the town's hotel from 1886 to 1888, when Anton Matty came into the picture. Matty rented from Rich until he was able to buy the hotel, livery stable, and saloon in 1896.

The son of Francois and Teresa (Colombet) Matty, Anton was born in 1840 in the Maritime Alps of France. His mother was a sister of Clemente Colombet, a Santa Clara Valley pioneer. He arrived at Mission San Jose after crossing the plains with an uncle whom he had met in the East upon coming to America as a boy of twelve. He remained with another uncle, Clemente Colombet, who built the Warm Springs resort near Mission San Jose, until 1885, when he went into business in San Francisco.

In 1866 he married Miss Sarah Slomon, an Irish girl, who died in November 1903, a few months after their son, Louis, had perished tragically in a forest fire near Wright's Station. Their other five children were Teresa, who was killed in an accident at the age of 18; Frank, who married Katherine Goodman; Thomas C., who died when he was 26; Annie Meyer; and Alice Matty.

Matty was an organizer of the Wright's school district and a member of the Santa Clara County Pioneer Association. He was also a member of the Sempervirens Club, one of a small group of citizens credited with having saved the Big Basin redwoods. He died April 12, 1922, at the age of eighty-two.

When she was still a young girl, Alice Matty became the fifth
station agent at Wright's. E. B. Green was the first, followed by Frank L.
Donahue, W. J. Van de Mark, Clare Hunter, Alice Matty, W. H.
Harrison, Jack Malone, and finally E. B. Crichton who remained in the
job until the station was closed July 16, 1932 despite bitter protests by
the residents of the region.

An asthma sufferer, Charles Henry Squire came to Wright's to
clerk in the store, then run by Ralph Thompson, in 1892. He worked
there until his brother bought the place two months later. In 1901,
James A. Squire sold the store to J. H. Garrity, and Charles Squire was
placed in charge until he bought out his employer in 1906. The great
earthquake of 1906 wrecked the store, and Squire was able to save only
a few odds and ends with which to start up again. He became postmaster in 1906 and held the job until 1923, when he moved away. He was
also a school trustee.

(Author's note—The post office was discontinued in 1938 with M.
A. Martin as the last postmaster, last of a line that started with Judge S.
P. Hall in 1883, Ralph Thompson in 1887, James A. Squire in 1893,
John Garrity in 1900, and Charles Squire in 1906. After the railroad
stopped running in 1940, all of the property around the station was
acquired by the San Jose Water Company, which cleared the site of all
of its buildings. Nothing remains today but the overgrown tunnel
entrance and the iron-railed bridge built in 1907. The tunnel was
closed with explosives during World War II.)

Wright's Station and Sunset Park

"Wright' s—A small village but an important shipping point, the
depot for the extensive fruit-growing sections of the surrounding
mountains. About 3200 acres of bearing trees and vines are in the
vicinity. Wild game and deer are numerous and occasionally black
bears (sic) are seen. Quail are plentiful and trout are in every
stream. . . . The Hotel Jeffries is a prominent resort and the Summit
Hotel, kept by Mrs. Nichols is another."

This note from an old county history published in 1893 gives an
interesting if not entirely accurate view of Wright's Station before its

Tourists in front of the Wright's Station Hotel, c. 1900.

turn-of-the-century heyday. Black bears were never found in the Santa Cruz Mountains, only grizzlies, and they had been extinct for many years before that history was published.

However, Wright's was indeed an important shipping center, serving the entire Loma Prieta region, Wright's ridge, Summit, and the district north to Alma. Hundreds of cars of fruit, grapes, and other produce and freight were shipped out of the station during the season. Wagons lined up for blocks in every direction at train time all summer, filling the flat in the middle of the village.

But it was the picnic idea that gave the place real impetus and put it definitely on the map for a lively decade. Sunset Park, soon to become one of the most popular of California's outing parks, was established at Wright's by the Southern Pacific late in the 1890s and almost immediately caught on, attracting hordes of visitors on weekends, holidays, and even during the week.

As many as four to five thousand people flocked to the village on occasion between 1900 and 1910. The Native Sons, the Foresters, and members of other lodges held meetings there, often rending the peace and quiet of the village with their merriment for days on end. Sunset Park soon became "the place" to come for picnic parties, weekend camps and summer outings. The hotel did a land-office business; cabins and cottages for rent blossomed on the hillsides.

The railroad ran three and sometimes four sections from Los Gatos and Santa Cruz, the former connecting with excursion trains from San Francisco, Oakland, San Jose, and way points. Horse-drawn stage-coaches and, later, wheezing automobiles raised a huge pall of dust on the winding mountain roads leading to the resort. But the fate of other mountain resorts of the era was also the story of Wright's—doomed by the coming of age of the automobile. Family automobiles began to carry vacationers to other, hitherto less accessible places of interest, such as Yosemite, Lake Tahoe, and beach resorts up and down the coast.

In this respect, the demise of Sunset Park was perhaps premature, and it might have survived until the advent of Prohibition had it not been for other, less obvious factors. One was competition from other resorts, especially the beaches. Another was a long series of complaints from ranchers along the route. It seems that the excursion trains made frequent stops along the way for the passengers to pick wildflowers and to perform other necessary functions. Evidently they did not confine their picking to wildflowers, nor were they careful with their litter.

Perhaps the railroad, starting to lose money on the trips, only wanted a good excuse to shut down the operation anyway. For whatever reason, Sunset Park was abandoned and Wright's began its long decline to oblivion. The fruit industry suffered from severe competition from burgeoning Valley orchards with lower shipping costs and easier production, and the wine grape industry collapsed overnight with the advent of Prohibition in 1919.

The Wright's Rifle Club

With the decline of Wright's passed one of the most colorful of the mountain's institutions, the Wright's Rifle Club, which numbered some of the world's most famous marksmen among its many members. In existence from about 1905 until 1915, when World War I shattered its ranks, the club was organized and first headed by John Utschig, president of the Austro-German colony in Austrian Gulch, on the slopes of Mt. Umunhum east of Wright's Station. Utschig at one time was a world champion rifle marksman.

The 200-yard range was situated on a hillside near the town, where meets were held the second Sunday of each month and impromptu tournaments were held at other times. The club was devoted to target shooting and often saw on its range masterpieces of craftsmanship equipped with all sorts of gadgets.

Holder of the 100-shot record was W. F. Blasse, San Francisco police marksmanship instructor, who with his brother, Martin, was a frequent visitor to the range. Another famous character often seen there was W. G. Hoffman, a San Francisco diamond setter whose hand was so fine, his admirers claimed, he once carved the Lord's Prayer on the head of a pin.

The Village of Burrell

The village of Burrell enjoyed but a brief existence as a community in the late 1890s and the early part of this century, but its telephone exchange (still in operation in 1934) gave it an importance far beyond its size.

Never dignified with a post office, the village consisted of a blacksmith shop and a store situated between the Burrell ranch and the old James Wright home, as well as a schoolhouse which came later. The Santa Cruz Mountain Telephone Company's central office at Burrell, however, provided a priceless service to its forest-bound subscribers, giving them their only means of contact with the rest of the world in times of emergency—sickness, accident, childbirth, and the ever-present menace of fire.

The founder of the community, for whom it was named, was Lyman J. Burrell, who with Charles McKiernan and John Martin Schultheis was one of the three earliest settlers in the region.

Born in Massachusetts in 1801, Burrell left his Ohio farm for the California mines in 1849. He became ill on the way home for a visit, having contracted fever crossing the Isthmus of Panama, and was unable to return to California until 1852. With his wife, the former Clarissa Wright, he took up farming on the lands of Cary Peeble and James Lick (for whom Lick Observatory was named).

In June of the following year, he and a group of friends took up land along the summit of the Santa Cruz Mountains, between Burrell and Los Gatos Creek, believing it to be government land open to homesteading. Six years later the land was found to be part of the great Rancho Soquel Augmentation, an enormous old Spanish and Mexican land grant.

In a lawsuit with the Castro heirs, descendants of the original grantees, Burrell emerged with 3,500 acres, a 1/27th share of the rancho (1/3rd of 1/9th), in partition. The suit was typical of the time, one of thousands of similar legal tangles that clogged the court dockets all over California for nearly a century. It was the result of the incredible carelessness with which the old Spanish-California families regarded their almost priceless land holdings and of surveys by untrained and sometimes almost illiterate surveyors.

Burrell's share of the rancho resulted from a formal division or partition made in 1863 by Thomas W. Wright, John W. Turney, and Godfrey B. Bockins as referees for the U.S. Land Commission which had been appointed by President Abraham Lincoln to settle such disputes. The partition was intended as final settlement of a legal fight that had started eighteen years before, when a tract of some 32,000 acres had been granted to Dona Martina de Castro by the Mexican government.

Rancho Soquel

Martina was the daughter of José Joaquin Castro, grandson of one Joaquin Castro, who had migrated to California from Spain prior to 1780. The grandson was the grantee of Rancho San Andreas in 1833, the same year that his daughter, Martina, was given Rancho Soquel and his son, Rafael, received the Aptos grant. In 1844 Martina received the famous Soquel Augmentation grant, and the fun began.

Martina, the widow of a member of the old Cota family, took for her second husband Michael Lodge, a Dublin sailor who had been shipwrecked on the Monterey coast in 1822. Lodge was killed by bandits in 1849 while en route home with a small fortune he had made by operating a pack train in the mining area. (A son, Michael, died in Santa Cruz in 1931, at the age of 93.)

It was probably at the suggestion of her husband, who seemed to have had an eye for marketable timber, that Martina applied for her two grants, which were made in her maiden name. The first, Rancho Soquel, totaled more than 1,668 acres, but Martina and her husband found that confining. Her second grant, the so-called Soquel Augmentation, contained 32,702 acres. Both grants later were confirmed by the U.S. Land Commission.

After the death of her second husband, Martina divided her land into nine equal parts, one for each of her eight children and the ninth for herself. On October 31, 1853, she conveyed her share in the old Rancho San Andreas to one Jane Smith. On January 22, 1855, she sold her remaining interest in the Soquel Augmentation to John Llebaria and John Ingoldby.

The last transaction proved to be her downfall. She evidently sold the tract to acquire a dowry for her impending marriage to one Louis Depaux, who turned out to be a deserter from the French Foreign Legion. Depaux persuaded Martina to sail with him to the Hawaiian Islands, but upon their arrival there he was arrested and sent back to France. Destitute, Martina returned to Santa Cruz to spend the remaining years of her life with a daughter, Maria Guadalupe Averon. She died in 1890.

Martina's sanity was repeatedly questioned and several efforts were made to have the partitions set aside. Innumerable transfers of the property brought other interests to bear, and the case remained in the courts almost down to the present time (1934). The litigation involved all the land between Loma Prieta ridge, with Loma Prieta as its northeast corner, west to the lagoon on the old McKiernan ranch above Glenwood, and south to the present town of Capitola. Included was some of the finest timber in the Coast range, valued in the multiple millions.

Martina's seven daughters and one son, original heirs to the land from their mother, were: Nicanor Cota, who married Francois LaJaunesse; Maria Louisa Cota, who married Ricardo Fordace Juan; Carmelita Lodge, who married Thomas Fallon of historical fame; Marita Josefa Lodge, who married Lambert Clements; Maria Helena Lodge, who married Joseph Littlejohn; Maria Guadalupe, who married Jose Averon; Antonia Miguel Lodge; and Michael Lodge.

Final partition of the Soquel ranch proper was made in 1860 by Referees C. B. Younger, David Tuttle, and Joseph Ruffner, who determined the land to cover 2,800 acres. Frederick A. Hihn, czar of Santa Cruz, received 404 acres. Part of Hihn's interest was from Joseph L. Majors and his wife, Maria de Los Angeles Castro, a sister of

Martina, who had claimed 1/8th prior to 1856 when they mortgaged
their portion along with their home.

Under the Augmentation partition, Lyman J. Burrell received
1/27th; Frederick A. Hihn 12/19ths; Ricardo Forcade Juan and his wife
1/27th on Valencia Creek including a coal mine. John H. Shelby and
R. H. Hinkley (for whom Hinkley Gulch was named) jointly received
1/36th including a sawmill. John Daubenbiss received 1/18th including
a sawmill in which he was interested with John Hames. Daubenbiss
bought the interest of George W. Evans in the mill.

Other awards included: Thomas P. Fallon and his wife, Carmelita,
of San Jose, 1/9th; Henry W. Peck and wife, 5/27ths; Joseph Littlejohn
and wife, 2/27ths; Augustus Noble, 120 acres; Richard Savage, 1/96th;
Jose Averon and wife, 1/9th; George K. Porter, 2/27ths; Benjamin
Farley, 1/48th; James Taylor of San Jose, 1/54th; Casimero and Dario
Amaya, jointly, 1/27th; John Bates, 1/27th on Bates Creek including a
sawmill; Cravel P. Hester of San Jose, 1/48th.

From this roster of names, many of them already famous, it is
evident that history was in the making in this litigation; land holdings
that later became the foundation of fortunes changed hands. Many
previously obscure figures who later became illustrious in state history
appeared for the first time on documents in the Santa Cruz County
courthouse.

Many of the faded and yellowed documents are in Spanish, full
of the flowery circumlocutions so dear to the hearts of early-day
California Castilian barristers.

The Burrells

Lyman J. Burrell engaged in stock raising for several years, raising
swine and goats, but the grizzly bears and cougars played such havoc
with his stock he was forced to turn to long-horned cattle, which were
better able to defend themselves. In this latter enterprise he had a
partner named John A. Quincy.

Before the establishment of the post office at nearby Patchen in
1872, the nearest post office to Burrell was at Santa Cruz, where Lyman

Burrell, like his neighbors, McKiernan and Schultheis, traveled by mule train over the old trail for mail and supplies.

Still virgin timber at the time, the terrain was without brush cover under the giant trees, making travel fairly easy through the park-like landscape. The most direct route often proved to be the best route, without regard to established trails. After five years of this kind of travel, Burrell built a wide trail along the Summit ridge, a route that later was acquired by the San Jose Turnpike Company in 1862 for its new stage road to Soquel.

Burrell sold off his land piecemeal right up to the time of his death on June 3, 1884, when he had but 1,000 acres left. County records show that he sold to Martha A. Burrell, a daughter, a portion of the Soquel Augmentation grant for $50; another portion to his son, J. B. Burrell, for $1,000; and by deed of gift conveyed to his daughter, Clarissa, 60 acres on Burrell Creek.

His wife died in 1857, leaving three children: James Burney, Martha, and Clarissa (Clara), the latter the wife of Hiram C. Morrell. Burrell married again in 1864, this time to Mrs. Lucy Lewis who died in 1875; and a fourth time in 1876 to Mrs. Filomena Vining.

The only surviving member of the original family is Martha A. Burrell, daughter of Lyman J., who is now (1934) living in Oregon with a niece, Mrs. Harry Morton, wife of a district judge. At 91 years of age, she has a remarkably clear memory and is able to recount many events of the early days in the Summit region.

The Morrells

Hirman C. Morrell, a miner and lumberman who married Burrell's daughter Clarissa, was a native of Maine, born in 1835. He followed the Gold Rush to California in 1854, and worked in the mines for six or seven years.

About 1860 he came to the Santa Cruz Mountains to run a sawmill for Howe & Weldon in what is now called Aldercroft Canyon, and the next year went to work for McMurtry & McMillan (Young) on Los Gatos Creek near Lexington, where he stayed four years. In April 1867,

Morrell bought the present-day Morrell ranch property and later acquired timber and a sawmill in Santa Cruz County.

He married Clarissa Burrell in 1864 and had five children: Lizzie M., Clifford H., Jesse B., Minnie C., and Albert E. Morrell. He died in San Jose in 1924.

Morrell was followed to the mountains by his brother, E. Bradford Morrell, who had pioneered hydraulic mining in the Sierra Nevada foothills in the early 1850s. Brad, as he was known, was the millman of the two. Hiram preferred ranching but worked with his brother in logging ventures from time to time.

Together (or Brad alone) they cut some of the finest timber in the Santa Cruz Mountains, including the early San Francisco mill site at the head of the San Lorenzo River. From there they transported their logs by flume to Felton before the logging railroad was built. Their second mill site was on the McKiernan property near present-day Glenwood, before they moved to the present site of Laurel and finally to several locations around Boulder Creek. Brad died a tragic death— run down by a runaway horse driven by a half-witted boy at a Fourth of July celebration in Boulder Creek in 1903.

The Wrights

Related to the Burrells by marriage, and neighbors in Ohio, were Mr. and Mrs. James Richard Wright, among the most prominent of Santa Cruz Mountain families.

Wright, a retired minister, and his wife, Sarah Vincent, daughter of a Boston family, came to the mountains in 1870 to settle on a 48-acre tract of land they were given by Lyman J. Burrell in settlement of an old debt.

Wright died in 1896; his wife in 1908. Their old home, still an imposing structure in (1934), was rebuilt after a fire in the 1890s. It and the modernized Burrell ranch home are the principal buildings in the tiny village of Burrell, along with the Wrights Presbyterian church.

A store built and operated for years by H. D. Ingram has been closed in recent years, as has the blacksmith shop built in the 1890s by E. T. Smith. The old Burrell school still stands (1979) half a mile east.

The old Burrell schoolhouse in 1979.

The telephone exchange, moved from Wright's Station, is still (1934) the focal point of activity in the region. It represents the second attempt to provide telephone service in that once-remote area. The first was a private line built by E. E. Meyer from his home place on Loma Prieta Avenue to Wright's Station in 1883, but too-accurate shooting by small boys with slingshots wreaked havoc with the fragile glass insulators on the line of poles, and the line was abandoned after four years.

It was not until 1909–10 that the telephone came to the mountains to stay, with the organization of the Santa Cruz Mountain Telephone Company by E. E. Meyer, Herman Grunsky, and Bob Borello. The first line, opened in January 1910, ran from the saloon at Wright's Station to Mare Vista, the Meyer winery, and way points, with twelve subscribers. Two more lines were added, to Ingrams and to Skyland; two more to the Summit area and Laurel; and another serving outlying ranches to make up the seven now in operation (1934).

Bohemia

Burrell was well supplied with roads early in its history, since it lies on the route of the San Jose Turnpike (Soquel Road), which abandoned its run over the Morrell cut-off in favor of the easier Comstock grade via Hall's Bridge. The old cut-off is still used but is in bad repair. It runs past a large tumbledown barn used for housing Japanese laborers during the fruit harvest.

Loma Prieta Avenue, running past the Wright place and the Smith residence to serve a line of ranch driveways, joins the main Loma Prieta Road above the Goldman ranch, "Villa Bergstedt."

For years the road was known as "White Wash Alley" because of its double row of white-washed fences bordering it for miles, despite the almost tearful protests of the resident poet, Josephine Clifford McCrackin, who would have preferred to see lichen-covered rail fences or none at all. (A later chapter gives further details on this area).

On Loma Prieta Avenue, just above the church, still stands (1934) a peculiar-looking structure with a high tower, often photographed as a curiosity by tourists. (Author's note—The tower has since been removed.) Within its walls, however, literary history was made.

This was "Bohemia," famous resort of the early part of this century, owned by Mr. and Mrs. Z. A. Cotton. It was a favorite haunt of Jack London, George Sterling, Ambrose Bierce, and the eccentric poet Herman Scheffauer. These and other well-known characters arrived at Wright's Station and either walked or took the stage to Burrell and Bohemia.

Austrian Gulch and Germantown

Along the western slopes of the Sierra Azul (Umunhum Ridge) and across Los Gatos Creek from Wright's Station where the headwaters of Austrian Creek and several other streams find their source, a handful of Austrian and German refugees from the Franco-Prussian war of 1870–71 attempted to establish a colony early in the 1870s.

Driven from their mother countries by the famine and poverty that followed the war, a dozen families under the leadership of John Utschig found their way into one of the remotest reaches of the Santa Cruz Mountains. Naturalized citizens all, they took up under U.S. government patents a dozen parcels of land in one of the best-watered sections of the Mountains, and one of the most beautiful.

Their guiding spirit was Utschig, who at the time he left Europe was acclaimed as the world's champion rifleman. His accomplishments with firearms were phenomenal. Others in the undertaking were B. Ernest Tittle, Lillan F. Ash, Ernst Essmann, Mary Catherine Wehner, Rudolph Huttula, Joseph C. Tittle, Ferdinand Koloday, Ulrich Rememsperger, Christopher von Staden, Frederick W. Grabau, and Wilhemina Huber.

These people and their holdings formed the nucleus of the colony, which depended for its existence upon extensive vineyards and a community winery which was soon erected in the heart of the 1,000-acre tract. A branch off of the old county road to Loma Prieta from Wright's Station was soon constructed, and before many years wagon loads of wine became a familiar sight on the loading platform at Wright's. Other immigrants followed—German, Italians, Austrians, Swiss—all to take up homesteads along the Sierra Azul from Mt. Hooker (now Mt. Thayer) to Mt. Bache (now Loma Prieta).

But the soil was thin—too thin for the intensive cultivation required for raising wine grapes. Competition from enormous Valley vineyards began to undercut the market for wine and wine grapes, and the whole project was already on the verge of economic ruin when the crippling blow fell.

The skies opened one winter night in 1889 and the rain came down in a cloudburst of the kind known only too well to long-time residents of a region where seventy inches of rain have been recorded in one season. Bubbling creeks became raging torrents. Solid walls of water moved down the steep mountain slopes which had been stripped of their natural cover, washing before them orchards, vineyards, and the homes of the settlers. How the people escaped—if they all did—is not a matter of record.

With a thunderous crash the big winery went down, taking with it the great vats and their contents of thousands of gallons of wine. Los Gatos Creek ran red with claret as far as Campbell, it is said, a tragic token of the blasted hopes of the little colony.

Although the orchards and vineyards were replanted and the winery rebuilt, the colony was on the decline. Some of the families returned to Europe; others left for the valleys and cities, and only a few clung to their hard-won holdings. Utschig, who moved to Wright's Station for a time, died in San Francisco in 1920.

Forest and brush fires repeatedly swept the slopes of the Sierra Azul, unimpeded by organized fire fighters as late as 1923, and destroyed most of the remaining structures. Other fires and floods accounted for the balance. By 1934, no trace remained of the picturesque little village of Austrian Gulch and the half-legendary hamlet of Germantown. Today (1934) all of the thousands of acres of the original colony are claimed by E. E. Cochran, San Jose attorney and one-time Wright's resident, and is the subject of a protracted lawsuit over rights-of-way between Cochran and the San Jose Water Company. (Author's note—All of the area described here is now closed to the public for watershed protection by the San Jose Water Company. The waters of Lake Elsman backed up behind Austrian Dam cover the sites of the forgotten villages.)

Settlers on the Ridge

Here and there along the ridge from Mt. Umunhum to Loma Prieta, and from there to Mt. Madonna, still other homesteaders made valiant but futile efforts to scratch out a living from the rugged terrain, mostly as individuals.

Nothing is left of their homesteads, but their names have persisted on maps and in the records, as place names do. For example, whoever named Nibs Knob, a dome-like peak on Loma Prieta Ridge at the headwaters of the Uvas, is no longer known. He is said to have been a druggist who tried ranching and failed.

The Knob (or Nob) adjoins a beautiful park-like flat watered by several springs called Maymen's Flat. This was the home for many years of Charles and James Maymen, early ranchers about whom little is known, except that they homesteaded the flat in the 1890s.

This also was the home of Hans and Herman Goertz and their families. Poverty-stricken to the last degree, they lived in a house so flimsy it threatened to fall down in every storm. Many times the families took to the brush when the weather became violent, lest the roof collapse upon them.

The children were without shoes, and their mother improvised footwear out of sacks in the intervals between charitable donations. Tragedy struck one night, and an incident of heroism is recorded that is one of the legends of the Mountains.

One of the Goertz children became ill, and although it was not known at the time, was suffering from acute appendicitis. No doctor was available short of San Jose at the time. Frantic in her extremity, the boy' s mother strapped the child on the back of a burro and led the animal by a rope over rough terrain at night, down the mountain and across the valley to a hospital more than twenty miles away—a trip that would have daunted a professional packer. The boy died a few hours after reaching San Jose, his appendix having burst on the terrible journey.

Beyond the Knob, toward Loma Chiquita, was the home of one of the most eccentric characters of the region, a Dr. Keinbortz, hermit and misogynist. A Civil War navy veteran, he transformed a tiny mountain valley into a paradise of flowers, with huge azaleas as the predominant bloom. He called the place "Glen Azalea," a scene of striking beauty. Only to" God and the flag" would he doff his hat, "not to any woman," he avowed, but this stand did not dissuade many of the women of the region from visiting his valley to admire the wealth of fragrant blossoms. His home burned down about 1924 or 1925 and Dr. Keinbortz moved away. Remnants of the fabulous gardens bloomed sporadically for years.

North and west along the Umunhum ridge lived several pioneer families whose names still appear on maps: Riley's spring, Cattermole ridge, Garrity ridge.

Hugh Riley was a retired Southern Pacific employee who built a house of corrugated iron on top of the ridge. The "Iron House" became such a well-known landmark that the ridge itself was called "Iron House Ridge." It was near the home of the Isenmingers.

Close by was the imposing home of the Cattermoles (also spelled Cathermola), now (1934) only a crumbling structure behind the towering chestnut trees that once lined the road from Wright's to the Summit. (Author's note—Cathermola Road still appears on road maps as a private road leading from Austrian Dam to Mt. Elizabeth.) Charles, John, and Henry Cattermole, three brothers from Bremen, lived there from 1886 until about 1900, operating a winery and a distillery, of which nothing remains today. A cabin on the same ridge was owned by one Harry Windell, who burned to death in his shack one night.

Garrity ridge was named for an early-day settler who had a cabin at the head of Los Gatos Creek above present-day Williams reservoir. Nothing is known about him.

Out on Loma Chiquita a Colonel Loveland and a man named Schemmel attempted to start a summer resort, but it failed. Loma Chiquita also was the site of another ill-fated attempt by Frank Thole to establish a summer colony known as Thole Heights.

Caught one winter by a storm when he remained too long at his mountain-top subdivision where he was working, Thole found himself unable to get out because the storm had destroyed his road. Suffering from exposure and his supplies running low, Thole contracted pneumonia. He lay helpless in his cabin for two days and nights before a fire ranger came to his rescue.

The ranger had driven up to Loma Prieta to check the lookout tower for storm damage, and looking over the ridge spotted a thin plume of smoke arising from the chimney of Thole's cabin. Knowing something must be wrong, the ranger hiked to the cabin and carried Thole out on his back to his car, and drove him to a San Jose hospital. Thole died there a few days later.

Loma Prieta—The Moving Mountain

Landmark for the surrounding country, Loma Prieta (dark ridge) towers 3,800 feet above sea level, the highest peak in the Santa Cruz range, now (1934) the site of a state forestry fire lookout.

Originally the peak was known as Mt. Bache, named for a U.S. Coast & Geodetic survey official who first recorded it on government maps. Under a curious error, the peak appears on some old maps as Mt. Umunhum, the name of another peak five airline miles to the north, but with the change of name to Loma Prieta the error was corrected.

Incidentally, origin of the name Umunhum is obscure, but it is probably of Indian derivation and is spelled several ways. The book *California Place Names* suggests the name may mean "resting place of the hummingbirds."

Believe it or not, Loma Prieta is not where it used to be when the first settlers homesteaded its flanks. In fact, between 1850 and 1934 the peak moved about twenty feet northeast.

According to Dr. Bailey Willis, Stanford geologist who measured the meandering mountain's movement in 1930, the peak travels about six feet every twenty-five years in the general direction of Morgan Hill.

The motion alarmed geologists at the time of the 1906 earthquake, and for a time thereafter a beacon flashed at regular intervals from its summit to an observation point on the coast, where the University of California maintained an earthquake station for the purpose. The beacon duly recorded the movement, but since nobody could do anything about it, the study was dropped.

According to Dr. Willis,"Loma Prieta is an outstanding example of a mountain moving. It has a wedge-shaped bottom, like the prow of a ship, pointing north. Pressure against it from the Pacific Ocean forced it toward the northeast and also raises it up in the air. It is not, however, moving at a rate that should disturb real estate values."

Dr. Willis estimated that the peak would reach Morgan Hill in about 25,000 years.

Along White Wash Alley

While the futile efforts to colonize other parts of the Loma Prieta region were failing in the latter part of the 1800s, a less concentrated German colony was springing up along what is now known as Loma Prieta Avenue, east of Burrell, and beyond. It brought to the mountains a notable gathering of world-famed artists, musicians, professional people, all in search of peace after the travail of the Franco-Prussian War.

From the intersection of Mt. Bache Road (as it was then called and as it still appears on some maps) with Spanish Ranch Road and Highland Way near Hall's Bridge, all the way to the summit of the Loma Prieta ridge, natives of Germany and their family settled in the 1880s and the 1890s.

Most of them are gone now (1934) and only a few of the members of the second generation have remained in the mountains. Their farms have been abandoned for a variety of reasons, or converted into summer homes and weekend retreats. Others have succumbed to fire, flood, or the intrusion of the forest.

A notable exception is Emil Meyer, son of E. E. and Marie Detje Meyer, who were among the first settlers along Loma Prieta Avenue and whose winery, "Mare Vista," is widely known. With the repeal of Prohibition, Meyer is regaining fame for his wines, grown from the celebrated mountain grapes which once provided the principal livelihood of the region.

A native of Denmark, E. E. Meyer married a German girl, Marie Detje, and settled in the San Francisco Bay area in 1874. For several years he ran a florist shop in San Francisco, then a business in San Jose, and finally moved to the Santa Cruz Mountains in the 1880s.

Meyer purchased 1,672 acres of the old Rancho Soquel Augmentation from Lyman J. Burrell, built thirteen miles of road through it, and soon became one of the leading citizens of the region.

The winery barn at Mare Vista.

He later sold part of the property until now (1934) about five hundred acres remain in his ranch, with seventy-five acres in grapes.

One of the curiosities of the Loma Prieta region was Meyer's "air mail" system, in operation long before the advent of aviation.

Situated as he was on the far side of a deep canyon from Loma Prieta Road, where the rural mail carrier made his rounds, Meyer needed a way to get his mail without a long trip around the gulch. He rigged an endless cable around pulleys at both ends, one end at the mail box, the other end at his house. The mail box rode on the cable suspended from wheels. When the mail carrier arrived and filled the box, he gave it a little shove to start it on its way. Meyer wound it in on a large pulley made from an old carriage wheel, emptied it, and sent it back for the next load.

Meyer's neighbors, above him on Loma Prieta Road, included William and Lucie Ernst Schraubstadter, a retired opera singer and his wife. A native of Germany, Schraubstadter had won fame in the East before moving to St. Louis and then Santa Cruz. The couple owned a small farm purchased from Meyer.

Adjoining the Schraubstadter place was the home of Josephine Lessman prior to 1888. She later sold it to Gustav Witzel, a San Francisco business man. The two ranches comprised what was known as the Marks place, which eventually became Herman's Resort. It was one of the show-places of the region.

Among others who made up the nucleus of a fair-sized community were the Haesters, vintners of the 1890s who later sold out to John Miehl, the Gehres, the Schollys, Henry Moeller, and the Jensch and Dietken families. Most of these families are gone and forgotten.

Several other farms were situated along White Wash Alley (Loma Prieta Avenue). The Lomita ranch of Henry Woods of San Francisco, and Monte Paraiso, home of Josephine Clifford McCrackin, formed the southern end of the row of white-washed fences.

Then there were Henry and Sylvester Hite, builders; the Wilson family from Hawaii; the Williams, Carrs, Finnies, Goodwinds, Mansfields, Eccles, Reeds, and Baldwins; also Mr. and Mrs. Z. A. Cotton at Bohemia at the Burrell end of the road. Here also was the once famous Jeffries Hotel, a resort that drew its clientele from the railroad at nearby Wright's Station in the 1890s.

Among the best known of the Loma Prieta families was that of Dr. Edmund Goldman. Born in Schleswig-Holstein on the Rhine, Dr. Goldman graduated from the great universities of Heidelberg and Giesen, then came to America for postgraduate studies at Bellevue Hospital in New York.

Settling in New Orleans in the early 1850s, he gained wide fame in medical circles for his work in combating the terrible epidemic of yellow fever that swept the city. At one time he was president of the New Orleans board of education.

Serving with the Union forces in the Civil War, Goldman saw action under General Sherman, Admiral Farragut, and others. In 1878 he married Julia Bergstedt of Germany and moved to Monterey in Old Mexico where their two daughters, Inez and Juanita, were born.

The Goldman family arrived in San Jose in 1887, bought their present ranch site from Emil Meyer in 1890 and built their home there while Dr. Goldman practiced medicine in San Jose for three years. Until his death in 1910, Dr. Goldman conducted his Villa Bergstedt as a private convalescent home, although he had retired from active practice. Physicians, however, were few and far between in the mountains, and Dr. Goldman responded to many an emergency call from far-off ranches where broken limbs, child-birth, and sudden illness only too often would have ended in tragedy had it not been for his services.

Terrible roads in blinding rain made no difference to the gods of chance. On one occasion Dr. Goldman was summoned in the middle of the night by John Miehl, ten miles away at Nibs Knob, to attend Miehl's father, who was dying of pneumonia. The errand was in vain; the old man was dead when Dr. Goldman arrived, but the doctor then was storm-bound at the Miehl ranch for two days. On another winter night, the doctor traveled through a wild storm to deliver a lusty pair of twins to the wife of a shoemaker named Nelson while the wind howled outside the cabin.

The Meyer Winery Fire

Wide World Magazine, in its issue of August 1900, devoted considerable space to an illustrated story on how a fire that threatened Mare Vista, the Meyer winery on Loma Prieta Road, was extinguished with wine.

By present-day literary or journalistic standards, it was a flamboyant account, prefaced with an editorial statement as follows: "We desire to draw particular attention to this remarkable account of American heroism and fertility of resource. How, when the Meyer winery was menaced the men turned to, fastened their hose to the wine vats, and averted destruction by pumping on the flames 4,000 gallons of wine."

There followed at length the story of the fire, one of the most destructive and tragic in mountain history up to that time.

In 1933 when the students at the Sacred Heart Novitiate at Los Gatos pumped thousands of gallons of wine on a fire to stop its spreading, the novelty of the action brought nation-wide publicity to the region. But it was not the first time: at Los Angeles in 1900 a planing mill fire was put out with Zinfandel wine from an adjoining warehouse; a few years earlier the Salazar winery at Mission San Jose was saved from fire by the same means. The unusual fire fighting method used at the Meyer Winery was not unique, but it was spectacular, as the account in *Wide World Magazine* illustrates: "During 1899 a dry season made fire particularly prevalent in California, and thousands of acres of forest were burned out owing to careless campers and sheepherders who believed that a forest destroyed by fire meant good fodder for the sheep the following year. Thus it is to these ignorant Basques, and to some ignorant Americans, that the destruction of some of the finest forests in California is due.

"The fire which swept over the Santa Cruz mountains on Oct. 8, 1899, was especially destructive, and to subjugate it the entire mountain community came to the front. . . . The fire, it was believed, was deliberately caused on the other side of the mountain by some irresponsible and even criminal individual who merely wished to burn some brush.

"A high wind, however, blew the flames forward, and in a short time a vast area was a raging site of fire. The moment it was seen that it was going to threaten life and property, the men of the mountains turned out en masse, hurrying to threatened ranches.

"By 2 o'clock E. E. Meyer and his son, Emil, were battling the flames on the adjoining ranch of the McCrackins, and also on Dr. Goldman's place, but the flames swept over the 50-acre timber tract, burning the ranch house and forest cottage on the McCrackin estate and driving the little band of fighters before them.

"Exhausted, the weary men turned to the threatened Meyer home, gathering about fifty fire fighters, not to mention women and children, for a last stand—men from Alma, from Soquel, and the entire mountain region.

"The roar of the flames was now so loud that men could not make themselves heard a yard or two away. The heavens were illuminated and vast columns of smoke arose so high they could be seen 50 miles away.

"There was not a fire engine for miles around and no appliances for fighting fire except the small hose used at the ranch. The men began to fear they, and their families, would soon be surrounded.

"The battle at Mare Vista was under the leadership of E. E. Meyer, and his son, and no force was ever led with better strategy. A few men happened to be on the scene when the fire swept upon the ranch. Ying, the Chinese cook, without orders collected all the kettles that would hold water, and at once an amateur brigade was formed, composed of Mrs. Meyer and some guests who tried to keep the flames from a ravine filled with trees near the winery.

"A fierce wind was now howling and the flames shot into the canyon like a fiery serpent and ate their way through it with incredible velocity. In a few minutes the winery was surrounded with a crescent of fire . . . the winery was evidently doomed.

"Trees blazing from top to bottom had plunged across the gulch, bridging it with flames, and the building was threatened on every side. A new danger soon became apparent. On the west was a small canyon into which the flames were seen eating their way with relentless force·

They came on with a roar, licking up the largest trees, and following up the driveway toward the house.

"The house was surrounded, but was saved by the fire fighters, partly by the heroism of Frank Murphy and others who crawled through the brush up Soquel Canyon and with a bucket brigade fought off the flames.

". . . Meyer and Albert Morrell were fighting the fire in a seething pit of pumice into which the flames had found their way below the winery. They were directing a stream into the red-hot vat, while above them in a window stood Emil Meyer, making it possible for them to work by turning a second stream of water on their persons.

"Suddenly a fierce gust sent a cloud of embers upon the roof of the scale-house, and in a moment it burst into blaze. There was no ladder at hand, but George Robeshot, who had fallen from the blazing McCrackin home earlier in the morning, made a flying leap for the roof at the risk of his life, and smothered the blaze with water-soaked blankets that were tossed up to him.

"Small buildings and outhouses now began to catch fire . . . and the men took their axes and tore down whatever they could. They were thus engaged when a cry of warning came. The pall-like cloud which had hung over the north end of the winery buildings, suddenly blew aside and disclosed the gasoline house smoking.

"In it were 100 gallons of gasoline, which, if it had exploded, would have destroyed every person in the vicinity. . . . It was necessary to break the connecting pipe from the winery. Albert Morrell climbed up to the engine floor and tried to break it, but failed. Emil Meyer heard his call and swung himself down from the winery roof. Then, single-handed, he broke off an iron pipe two men could not have bent under ordinary circumstances.

". . . the wind began to drive the flames in the direction of the water tank from which the men were obtaining their supply. A huge fir caught, blazed upward like a gigantic rocket, then fell with a terrible roar upon the tank, crushing it . . . along with the hopes of the brave band, while the flames came creeping ever inward.

"It was now that the resource—the genius—of Mr. Meyer as a fire-fighter was displayed. Attaching a hose unhesitatingly to the big wine vats, he shouted, 'Man the pumps!'

"Merrily rang the pumps, and by tapping one vat after another, no less than 4,000 gallons of claret were pumped onto the fire. The flames on the winery were finally subdued and by noon this extraordinary victory was won."

Some of the heroes of the battle were missing after the fight was over. "Since 2 o'clock in the morning every man had been fighting fire, with no food and no rest. Emil Meyer fell fainting across the threshold of his home and it was found that his clothes were almost burned from his body. George Robeshot was unable to reach the house and was found lying senseless in the yard. Frank Matty shouted that his brother had been overtaken by the fire, and a brave band of volunteers started in search of him. He was found lying exhausted where he had fallen, badly burned but alive."

That women played a no less valiant part in the battle is testified by an account of the pluck evinced by Inez Goldman, the sixteen year old daughter of the doctor. She rescued several horses from the barn after risking her life in a mad dash through the flaming brush. (Author's note—According to Emil Meyer's daughter, the winery was closed in 1939 after her father's death, and the big winery building was torn down a few years later. The property was then subdivided and several homes were built on acreage homesites.)

Josephine Clifford McCrackin

Poet and newspaper woman, friend and confidant of such illustrious characters as Bret Harte, Mark Twain, Charles Warren Stoddard, Ina D. Coolbrith, Joaquin Miller, Ambrose Bierce, Noah Brooks, and other writers on the famous old *Overland Monthly* when Harte was editor—this was Josephine Clifford McCrackin (sometimes spelled "en").

In the words of Ambrose Bierce, "Knowing her was a high privilege. She was a woman who had lived through and wrote of frontier days in the West after the Civil War, and who came to the

Santa Cruz Mountains to live and to become one of the region's most beloved residents." Her home at Monte Paraiso, on Loma Prieta Avenue (called White Wash Alley), which burned to the ground in the great forest fire of 1899, was the mecca for writers, musicians, and artists from all over the world.

Born in Germany in 1838 to a family in the nobility, McCrackin was raised in luxury. She and her family came to this country in the 1840s and settled in St. Louis, where her father died in 1854.

McCrackin's first marriage was to an American army officer, Lt. James A. Clifford, with whom she moved to Fort Union, New Mexico, when it was still a wild frontier post at the close of the Civil War. She later learned from her husband that he was wanted by the Texas authorities for a murder, which he claimed had been committed in self-defense. He appeared to lose his reason at this point and began to accuse her of betraying him. He threatened to kill her, but she escaped to San Francisco and never saw him again.

In California she started writing for the *Overland Monthly* and other magazines of the time under the name of Josephine Clifford, and soon became widely known. In 1882 she married Jackson McCrackin, a member of the Arizona territorial legislature and a well-known gold miner. A few years later they moved to the Santa Cruz Mountains and built Monte Paraiso.

They lived there until the fire of 1899 destroyed the famous home. When her husband died, in 1904, she found it necessary to go to work for a living, and joined the editorial staff of the *Santa Cruz Sentinel,* where she wrote some of the first articles to appear in the press urging the preservation of the redwoods. Later she joined forces with Andrew P. Hill, a noted San Jose photographer, and others in forming the Sempervirens Club, which was largely responsible for creating the California Redwood Park, which later became Big Basin State Park.

Mrs. McCrackin died in Santa Cruz in 1920, leaving behind her an enduring monument in the redwoods of Big Basin and an affectionate memory in the hearts of the mountain colony where she had lived and worked for seventeen years.

Skyland and Highland

An attempt to find a name signifying a place higher than high accounts for the present name of Skyland, an isolated community well up on the crest of the Santa Cruz Mountains, off Soquel Road in the Highland district.

Highland Hill was the original center of things here, the home of a man named Dodge, who in 1867 leased a tract of land from Lyman J. Burrell to establish a vineyard and winery. Later, as families moved into the district to join in the growing wine grape industry that spread through the hills in the late 1860s and 1870s, a colony adjoining Highland Center, as it came to be known, was labeled Skyland, although the two places are virtually identical.

Booming with the rest of the region, the town benefited principally from grape- and fruit-raising, and to a lesser extent from the lumber industry which went on around it in the canyons below. But as it benefited, so it suffered. The close of the lumber mills on the Soquel, Amaya, and Laurel Creeks as the big timber was cut off, the coming of the automobile that doomed the summer resort trade of railroad and stagecoach days, and the competition from the Valley with the mountain fruit crops all took their toll from Skyland, along with many another mountain town.

Phylloxera, the dreaded grape disease from France, wiped out large acreage in 1906 and 1907, just after the great earthquake had played such havoc with much of the region which lies directly over the San Andreas fault line. Erosion on the steep hillside ranches, where forest cover had been removed for planting, had set in after forty years of cultivation and was stripping the upper ridges of topsoil and filling the lower lands with its spoil. Springs were sealed over and many creeks had stopped running.

With nothing much left but a surprisingly mild climate and an unsurpassed view to offer in competition with more accessible towns,

Skyland began to fade early in this century, although the advent of good roads aided somewhat in its tenuous grasp on departed glories of the 1880s and 1890s.

Travelers, residents, and visitors alike found ready ingress and egress down the ridge to Hall's bridge and Soquel Road, over the hill to Redwood Lodge and Hester Creek, or down less-traveled routes into Asbury Gulch and across to Highland Way.

Here it was that Don Beadel, Pacific coast shipping magnate, came to purchase a large tract of land from F. A. Hihn and to establish The Willows ranch, above the site of the old McEwen-Adams lumber mill of the 1880s.

The Willows

Beadel's son, Alec, one of the three brothers who operated the Beadel Brothers shipping concern, started in about 1904 to build up the estate to a stage of affluence which makes it even today (1934) one of the showplaces of the entire mountain region.

Al Beadel married the daughter of a Mrs. Hold, who had acquired the land from Don Beadel, and brought the property back into the family. Cottages and a beautiful rambling central home on the style of English farm houses sprinkled the landscape, crowned with what was said to be the largest privately owned indoor swimming pool in the United States. Under a huge canopy of glass, the great double pool of concrete and tile brought the curious from miles around and occupied columns of space in Eastern newspapers of the period.

Exotic garden plants from all quarters of the globe were planted in profusion; grassy terraces, fountains, and rock gardens transformed the forest into a paradise. Acquired recently by a Fresno rancher, J. B. Enloe, the estate is now (1934) being renovated for eventual opening as a resort.

Skyland Notables

Skyland post office ceased to exist in 1910 after rural free delivery came to the mountains at the end of a long, hard fight by the ranchers

The famous indoor pool at the Willows resort.

of the region for the service. The post office then had been in operation over two different periods: 1884 to 1886, and 1893 to 1910.

In 1887 the pious people of the community erected a church, planting in the front yard a separate bell tower under a spreading oak tree. (Author's note—The church is still in use today, making it probably the oldest church in continuous use in the Santa Cruz Mountains.)

Skyland was also the home for nearly twenty years of Joseph James Bamber, one of the region's more colorful characters, whose death was marked by an obscurity no less remarkable than his career.

An "unidentified itinerant" knocked down by a car near the county alms house where he spent his last days brought only the briefest of notices in the newspapers at the time, March 19, 1930, when Bamber died in the county hospital from a fractured skull. He was later

Skyland Church, c. 1934. The tree has since been cut down.

identified as Joseph J. Bamber of Los Gatos, a former newspaperman, and that was that. Bamber had been the publisher of an unusual newspaper, called *The Mountain Realty*, which enjoyed a more or less continuous existence at Skyland for two decades, from 1901 until 1922 when it was absorbed by Hi Baggerly's *Los Gatos Mail-News*. Under a Skyland dateline, the paper was devoted to mountain news and real estate notes, circulating throughout the central Santa Cruz Mountains. At first, it was printed by the *Santa Cruz Sentinel*, later in Los Gatos. Advancing years finally forced Bamber to give up the paper.

Born in Illinois, Bamber had come to the West Coast as a young man and settled in the Bay region, where he engaged in a wide variety of enterprises.

An original cover in the philatelic collection of E. E. Place of Los Gatos bears the heading "Bamber & McLeod Express," a pony service running from Oakland to Centerville. Bamber at one time amassed a considerable fortune in the business, but lost it later.

The *Pacific Coast Business Directory* of 1872 lists the American House at Centerville, operated by Bamber, as one of the principal hostelries of Alameda County. In 1872 Bamber married Miss Virginia Hill of Oakland, said to be the first white child born in Oakland (in 1853). She died in 1917. The couple operated a laundry in Alameda for a time, then the famous old Newport baths near Neptune Beach, also in Alameda, then moved to the mountains in 1893, settling about where Holy City now stands. In 1895 the family moved to Skyland where they ran a small hotel, a ranch or two, and finally the newspaper which was Bamber's last enterprise.

Skyland in the early 1930s was also the home of James B. King, a pioneer of the 1880s with a lively sense of humor and a keen recollection of days gone by.

King was prouder of his one-time title of "Champion plowman of the world" than he would have been of Jack Dempsey's fame, he said. (King had won the championship plowman's title in an international competition in Chicago in 1880. He had previously won third place twice.) Indeed, Dempsey was a frequent visitor to the region, King declared. At one time, according to King, Dempsey was thinking of buying the Willows, but gave up the idea after his car got stuck in the mud several times in one winter.

One of his liveliest recollections was of an ill-fated trip to the Klondike in 1898. Following the story of an old prospector about a claim where all they had to do was to shovel out the gold, King and a group of friends bought an old tub on the San Francisco Bay mudflats, for $1,500, and somehow managed to get it to Resurrection Bay in Alaska.

Of the party, only four were experienced sailors, although all signed on as able-bodied seamen in order to obtain clearance under a Captain Edwards. Besides King, the party included M. R. Morse of San Jose; Julius Josefat and Clayton Jones of Skyland; John Rankan, Wayne Rudey and F. LaSalle of Soquel; Bill Peakes, Bob Baxter, Bob Anderson, Albert Wright, A. G. Imlay, Chauncey Lease, and A. W. Bryant.

The party spent eight months looking in vain for gold. The old prospector who was to lead them to the lode had inconsiderately died the day before the party left San Francisco. However, it was not all loss. On their return, they leased the boat to some missionaries for a year, and then sold it for $3,000 just before it went to pieces on the beach.

Skyland was a residential section of note in the 1880s and 1890s, numbering among its well-known residents Charles H. Allen, principal at San Jose State Normal School, and Professor Norton of the same school.

While several fine homes are still to be found in the community, the principal attraction at the present (1934) is the New Jerusalem Colony of Mr. Ernest Benninghoven, a strange religious cult which has struggled along for the last fifteen or twenty years with a handful of converts. Its center is the "Mt. Sinai Shrine," a memorial to the memory of Benninghoven, who departed this earth a few years ago.

The Hihn Empire

The story of Skyland would not be complete without the story of the man who owned most of the forests around the town and provided it with much of its livelihood, who paid at one time a reputed one-tenth of all the taxes in the county—Frederick A. Hihn.

Born in Germany in 1829, he landed in Santa Cruz with a pack on his back in 1851, after a series of business ventures and a mining attempt or two. In his pack were all his earthly possessions, plus some trinkets to sell as a roaming peddler. According to Herbert Martin of Glenwood, who recalled his father's stories about Hihn and his pack, Hihn set up business in a crude store constructed of packing boxes. Between tending his store and making long trading forays into the mountains, he was a busy man.

How he managed to acquire an enormous fortune in real estate, including thousands of acres of prime redwood timber, is one of the legends of the county. Among his holdings was a mill site at Laurel, where the Hihn company operated in 1892 with his sons, Louis W., August C., and Fred O. Hihn, and son-in-law, W. T. Cope.

Hotels, railroads, concessions, forests, mills, manufacturing plants and shipping lines—there was little in the line of business in Santa Cruz County that the Hihn company did not own or was actively involved in during this period. One Santa Cruz County history published in 1892 credits him with founding Capitola, along with a couple of banks.

The upper portion of his holdings in Soquel canyon, bordering on Skyland and Spanish Ranch, is still known as the Hihn forest.

Buffalo Jones and Frémont

It was not because he had shot so many buffalo that old Zachariah Jones was called Buffalo Jones—it was because he looked like a buffalo and roared like one, and doubtless smelled like one.

A character whose story has become a legend in the nearly ninety years (in 1934) since he arrived at the present site of Lexington, Jones was without a doubt one of the very first Americans ever to set foot in the Santa Cruz Mountains.

That Jones was already here when John C. Frémont came through with his scouting party in February, 1846, seems likely, although Frémont makes no mention of him in his journal, and some accounts place Jones' arrival a year or two later.

Jones himself, who probably was illiterate, left no journal, hence it is to "The Pathfinder," as Frémont was known, that we are indebted for one of the most complete descriptions ever written of the Santa Cruz Mountains in Jones's time. In his meticulous diary also is recorded the first account of the Lexington region. Exactly where Frémont and his party camped in the area is a matter of conjecture—a certain large oak tree at nearby Alma claiming the glory of having provided shade for the party, while above Lexington, near Idlewild, is an equally attractive spot that claims the honor.

It was in the latter spot, less than twenty years later, that Louis Hebard, who came to Alma in 1857, found a rusty spur and the remains of a saddle under a huge madrone tree—relics he treasured as mementos of the Frémont expedition.

This actually was Frémont's second crossing of the Santa Cruz Mountains on his so-called topographical expedition, which in reality was but a thinly veiled bit of opportunism on the part of the United States government to take a peek at this magnificent territory that all the world knew Mexico could no longer hold.

Whether topographical or frankly aggressive, the descriptions of the country in his diary are minute and present a vivid picture of this region. He wrote in part:

"Resuming the work of the expedition, on the 22nd February we encamped on the Wild-Cat (Los Gatos) ridge on the road to Santa Cruz and again on the 23rd near the summit. The various character of the woods and shrubbery on this mountain, which lies between my camp and the Santa Cruz shore, was very interesting to me, and I wished to spend some days there, as the spring season was now renewing vegetation, and the accounts of the great trees in the forest on the west slope of the mountain had aroused my curiosity.

". . . We remained on the upper portion of the mountain several days. The place of our encampment was 2000 feet above the sea, and was covered with a luxuriant growth of grass a foot high in many places.

"At sunrise the temperature was 40 degrees; at noon, 60 degrees; in the afternoon, 65 degrees; and 63 degrees at sunset, with very pleasant weather. The mountains were wooded with many varieties of trees, and in some parts with heavy forests. These forest are characterized by a cypress (*Taxodium*) of extraordinary dimensions, which I have already mentioned among the trees in the Sierra as distinguished among the forest trees of America by its superior size and height.

"This is the staple timber-tree of the county, being cut into both boards and shingles and this is the principal timber sawed at the mills. It is soft and easily worked, wearing away too quickly to be used for floors; but it seems to have all the durability which anciently gave the cypress so much celebrity. Posts which have been exposed to the elements of weather three-quarters of a century, since the foundation of the missions, showed no marks of decay in the wood and are now converted into beams and posts for private dwellings. In California the tree is called Palo Colorado, or red-wood."

(Frémont confused the *Sequoia sempervirens* of the coast with the *Sequoia gigantea* of the Sierra, and both with a variety of cypress. The error in classification was not discovered until 1847 by botanists, a year after Frémont's visit, although the tree had been described by Spanish explorers nearly one hundred years earlier).

"Among the oaks in this mountain is a handsome, lofty evergreen tree, specifically different from those of the lower grounds, and in the general appearance much resembling hickory. The bark is smooth, of a white color, and the wood hard and close-grained. It seems to prefer the north hillsides, where they are nearly four feet in diameter and 100 feet high."

(This was probably the tan-bark oak, *Lithocarpus densifiora*, which provided a major source of revenue for mountain people for half a century, when tanning hides was a major industry. Tanbark is still used to a limited extent in tanning).

"Another remarkable tree of these woods is called the rnadrone. It is a beautiful evergreen with large, thick and glossy digitated leaves; the trunk and branches reddish colored and have a smooth and singularly naked appearance, as if the bark had been stripped off. In its green state the wood is brittle, very hard and close-grained. It is said to assume a bright red color when dry, sometimes variegated, and susceptible of a high polish. The tree was found by us only in the mountains. Some measured nearly four feet in diameter and were about 60 feet high."

This was the verdant scene that greeted the eye of Buffalo Jones when he first came to the mountains, and this was the scene that he helped to destroy as he made his living out of fence posts and shingles, tanbark and cordwood.

Where he came from, and where he went when the place became too crowded with a handful of people later on, is a complete mystery. He lived with C. C. Martin at Glenwood for a time after Martin had built for him a small sawmill in 1852–53, about where the San Jose Water Works flume crosses Los Gatos Creek above Alma.

(Author's note—This site, along with the towns of Alma and Lexington, vanished under the waters of Lexington reservoir, built by the water company in the 1950s.)

Jones was a familiar sight in the mountains in the early years of white settlement, but after spending a few years with the Martins he pulled up stakes one day and moved on, and that was the last that was ever heard of him in these parts.

Jones's Road

Jones told both C. C. Martin and Louis Hebard, as well as others, that he had come in 1846 over a bear trail from the Valley, the same route over which he later packed in lumber and supplies for his lonely shanty that stood in the Lexington flat.

This "bear trail" was undoubtedly the Santa Cruz branch of El Camino Real, the route of the Spanish padres in their travels between the missions, and before them the trail of the Ohlone Indians for at least three centuries.

Swinging up over St. Joseph's hill of today, where the Sacred Heart Novitiate crowns the rise directly to the southeast of Los Gatos, the trail dropped precipitately down the south side of what is still known as Jones Hill into Lyndon Gulch, emerging just above the junction of the gulch with Los Gatos Creek, and crossing it to enter the flat where Lexington stands, two miles above Los Gatos on the Santa Cruz Highway.

Steep, rough, and in the summer a wondrous place for dust, the trail in winter was a dangerous place for pack trains and men alike. The bull teams that followed as well as the stage coaches with their iron-shod wheels, did little toward improving the route, simply transforming it into a pair of parallel ruts that provided a hair-raising ride for venturesome travelers.

Jones's road was the only pass over the mountains through the ridge of the cats (Los Gatos), and it was so steep that only half-loads could be carried on each trip. According to an account written by Mrs. Fremont Older in 1925, the pass was named Farnham's Pass for a Mrs. Farnham who was said to be the first woman to cross the Santa Cruz Mountains in a wheeled vehicle.

Residents of the Valley finally persuaded the county board of supervisors to build a new road, and two expeditions were sent out the following year—one over the mountains eastward into the San Joaquin Valley, the other over the Santa Cruz Mountains.

"Uncle Ike" Branham, famous hunter, and his pack of hounds spent a couple of weeks on the eastern route and returned to report it impractical. Then Sheriff John Murphy, a fine horseman, explored the

Jones Hill Road out of Los Gatos, c. 1934.

Santa Cruz gap with a party on horseback, reporting that it would cost $10,000 to build a road from Jones' road to the county line, and advised the purchase of Jones' road.

This plan was turned down, and the county found itself at an impasse, for the statute then in force which had been passed March 12, 1853, contained no proviso for building a toll road but merely authorized the formation of a corporation "for the construction of a plank or turnpike road."

In 1857, however, the law was amended to grant powers as follows: "All companies formed or hereafter formed have power to bridge any stream and determine all matters of construction such as width, manner, style, etc., but shall be only allowed to keep toll gates and collect tolls as fixed by the board of supervisors in each of the counties through which the roads pass, tolls to be paid from year to year."

With this power in hand, the supervisors granted to the Santa Cruz Gap Joint Stock Company permission to build a toll road from Los Gatos to the Summit. The officers were Adolph Pfister, president; D. B. Moody, secretary; and L. A. Whitehurst, E. H. Evans, R. S. Smith, A. S. Logan, and J. Y. McMillin.

The new road was first put to use May 5, 1858, when Joseph Johnson and Peter Davidson piloted the first wagon over the new route, according to Mrs. Older. This was the road that first traversed the western side of the canyon, following approximately the same route as the present highway (1934) as far as Alma, where it branches off past the old Forest House side and where a fire ranger station is now located, then followed Aldercroft road for a short distance before emerging again on the highway, then meandered in and out of the canyons, following lines of least resistance.

All was not serene, however. The first winter rains that came along washed out the new road, and to cap matters Jones continued to operate his old road in opposition. But lawsuits and prolonged wrangling wearied him and he finally sold out his rights to J. P. Henning and S. Thomas.

A portion of the old Jones road is still used occasionally by crews from the San Jose Water Works maintaining the flume line that follows it, and by students at the Novitiate out for a walk.

Land Disputes

Jones's peculiar methods, never clearly explained, of acquiring land (he apparently didn't bother to take-up homesteads, but simply squatted on all available territory and laid claim to all the redwood trees in sight) brought him into trouble quite often as later settlers disputed his titles. On one occasion (May 26, 1858) he sued Samuel Gummer, Edwin French, and John Stewart, and in another suit named Lafayette Jones, William Biddle, Eli Hopper, Dudley Wells, and Isaac Bird, charging that they all had "trespassed on his lands, cut his redwoods," and committed other damages to the tune of $1,000.

He claimed in his suits that the defendants had already cut one hundred trees on his mountain acres valued only for timber, on which he (Jones) had "erected sawmills and graded roads at a cost of some $18,000." He charged in particular that on May 18, 1858, French and Hugh E. Steele "entered on his land and cut timber and worked it into posts and rails which later were sold to Hanson and Howt" (probably Howe).

The defendants denied Jones's claims to title on the lands, alleging that they were in the public domain. The suit hinged on school land warrants which Jones held, but these were not admitted in evidence on the grounds that the surveys on which the warrants were based were "not made in accordance with survey laws."

An old parchment map on file at the Santa Clara County courthouse reveals that the surveys were based on comers that were trees—a large madrone, a small oak, etc., a common practice in early days, which obviously led to much trouble later.

The school land warrants, a curious form of land deed, were issued August 24, 1853, for 320 acres, and June 3, 1852, for 160 acres, under an act "to provide for the disposal of 500,000 acres" of land granted to the state by an act of Congress signed May 3, 1852. The original grantee on the first tract was William Walker, who assigned the land to Josiah Belden. The second tract was granted to Charles Hunspeth, who assigned it to Jones, for considerations which were not made public.

Silent Charley

"UPSET—The stage for Santa Cruz, on Thursday last, containing eight or nine passengers, upset about a mile beyond Mountain Charley's, and rolled down a gulch about 150 feet. The passengers luckily tumbled out, and no one was seriously injured. The accident was caused by some hogs rushing down the hill and jumping among the horses while making a sharp turn around a point, causing them to jump off the grade."

This account of a freak accident appeared in the weekly San Jose newspaper in 1865 and gives a graphic picture of what was then a more or less commonplace incident on the stage road and a firsthand view of the life of the times.

The hogs, incidentally, belonged to Mountain Charley McKiernan, and were more than half-wild. The accident took place at the curve at the head of Lynch hill, which was not named for the famous roping custom but for a "retired" blackbirder and ex-pirate, David Lynch, who had a little ranch in the area, according to the recollections of Herbert Martin from his father, who lived close by.

Among the amusing anecdotes of the road was one which describes the predecessor of the modern automobile horn—the teamster's throaty whistle. So narrow was the Jones road, and so sharp the turns, that encountering another team suddenly was as hazardous as meeting a speeding automobile on a narrow mountain road of today. As a warning, the drivers of that time were accustomed to sounding a blast with their lips as they approached each curve, a sound that carried an incredible distance.

This was the mountain scene when Lexington began back in the 1850s, and when Charley Parkhurst, noted stage driver and a typical character of the period, first appeared to make history in the Santa Cruz Mountains.

Charley's full story has never been told and probably never will be, but what little is known gives an intimate picture of the customs, manners, and a little of the dress of the times among that hardy breed—the stagecoach drivers. Almost nothing is known of Charley's early years, but from about 1868 on, Charley became one of the most famous of the drivers on the San Jose-Santa Cruz stage run.

Kicked in the face by a horse, Charley had lost one eye and wore a black patch over the socket. This patch, accompanied by habitually stained lips from an excess of tobacco chewing and a saturnine cast of countenance, made Charley as tough-looking as the most hardened and bewhiskered denizen of the mountains. Oddly enough, Charley went smooth-shaven, unusual for men of the period. Profane to the extreme, cold and unfriendly in manner, Charley presented every appearance of an odd but nonetheless typical "whip" of the 1860s. Until the day Charley died, nobody suspected that Charley was a woman.

She was born in 1812 under the name of Charlotte Parkhurst. She came to California in the early 1850s and drove a stage in the mining country, always masquerading as a man.

Like most knights of the overland stage, she wore a muffler, gloves, great-coat of buffalo hide, and a cap of the same material. Under this she wore blue jeans turned up to reveal the cuffs of a very good pair of trousers, according to Major A. N. Judd, whose recollections of Charley Parkhurst appeared in the *Santa Cruz Surf* on October 18, 1917. Major Judd said he had traced Charley's history back to the Indian days on the overland stage, where she made her first public appearance.

She learned her trade at a livery stable in Vermont, a job she obtained by pretending to be a young man, this according to another account written by John Royce of San Jose in the *Santa Cruz Sentinel* in 1917. Royce states that Charley rapidly became the most expert driver in the state first with two horses, then four, and finally six. She was always entrusted with driving parties requiring a showy, but careful driver.

According to Major Judd's account, Charley drove overland stage for three years for Ben Holiday out of Council Bluffs, Iowa. Judd's story of her experiences on this job still makes for lively reading:

"I suppose that here I should make a distinction between the Sioux, Blackfeet and others in the East, and the Indians that infested the western slopes of the Sierra,'for they all had their fling at Charley Parkhurst.

"Old Ben Holiday was the moving spirit in the Overland stage line. He had his office at Council Bluffs, Iowa. Monday morning was his busy day in hiring drivers to replace those whose hair had been raised either by fear or by the scalping knife.

"The Indians were not the most fearsome thing to dread, for on the mountain roads were the perils of the steep and narrow grade, so narrow that on some turns the singletree had cut grooves into the banks on the high side, and often the other side was a thousand feet down to the stopping place if the vehicle should go over.

"It was these dangers that also thinned out drivers fast, and the one under discussion that brought Charley into the limelight for the first time.

"There were perhaps 50 applicants for the positions that were open on the stage line.

"'Ever driven stage? How long? How near could you drive to the edge of a bluff with a sheer drop of a thousand feet with perfect safety to your self, your team and passengers?' These were some of the questions fired at the prospective drivers by Holiday.

"Many answered until nearer and nearer they got to the edge. Finally, one was willing to take a chance with half the tire over the edge on one wheel.

"About this time Charley's turn came around, and by this time he (she) was getting uneasy. After putting between her jaws a fresh chew, she closed her jackknife that had done duty for years not only for cutting tobacco but for mending harness or skinning a deer.

"She got up and had almost reached the door before saying over her shoulder, 'I wouldn't do at all for you, Mr. Holiday. I'd stay as far away from the edge of that cliff as the hubs would let me.'

"'You are just the man I want,'" said Holiday. "For three years Charley held that job without an accident, and would have stayed longer, but the Mormons were of a marrying disposition and rather than disclose her secret by marrying a few dames with polygamous proclivities, she left for the Pacific Coast. After a short spell on the Pacheco Pass run, she joined up with the Danforth Porter lines that connected with the Santa Cruz stage line.

"Charley was a great 'whip,' and when she pulled into a stage stop with the beautifully equipped 20-passenger Concord coach, drawn by six mustangs as mettlesome as quarter-horses, it was an inspiring sight indeed.

"Every move played its part. One would note with what dexterity she plied the brakes just tight in order to stop with the door just opposite the main entrance to the hotel.

"How deftly she whirled the six-horse lash around the stock and carefully laid it up on the deck, all unconscious of the onlookers, and as she wrapped the lines around the foot brake she would turn to hand down the treasure box or mail sack, or perhaps a venturesome female who had insisted on tiding with the driver."

Major Judd recalls how, when the teams were running all out, the stagecoach often would rock back and forth like a boat on its long, leather springs called "thorough-braces."

"Those springs each weighed 50 pounds, and their going price was a dollar a pound, thus a pair would cost not less than $100 each with its many leaves forming a long oval hoop forming a cradle for the body of the coach. With clamps and fasteners, they made riding as easy as a boat ride in a gentle swell and with more joy for the passengers."

But this romantic picture faded, Major Judd relates, when the railroad reached the Twelve Mile House (out of Santa Cruz) where Charley had a station on the Santa Cruz-Los Gatos road which was known as Sand Hill Station.

Out of the business of driving stage or tending a station, Charley began raising stock on Bean Creek. Between times she hauled for neighbors, until approaching old age made her infirm. She retired on money raised from the sale of her stock to Charley Moss of Moss Landing and lived for a time near the old Seven Mile House.

Her partner in the cattle venture was another "bachelor," Frank Woodward, and from time to time one or another of the two would work for Major Judd, hauling wood.

In her last days, Charley was attended, all unsuspecting, by a twelve-year-old son of the Harmon family named George, to whom Charley willed all her meager possessions in return for his kindness. The possessions amounted to about $600 deposited with Otto Stoesser in Watsonville.

Charley died in her lonely cabin in December, 1879, an event that created quite a furor. It was when she was "laid out" that it was discovered for the first time that Charley was a woman.

Charley's partner, Woodward, it is recorded, waxed profane to the extreme when he learned of the deception practiced on him for so many years.

Lexington Begins

Just when Jones's Mill ceased to be and Lexington began is not clear, but it was not long after California was admitted to the Union that the place began to be noticed as one of the booming communities of Santa Clara County. Certainly by 1867 it had become one of the County's most active centers of commerce, while its neighbor, soon to become Los Gatos, was known as Forbes Mill and was nothing but a dusty crossroads, a place one went through en route to Lexington.

Situated as it was two miles above Forbes Mill in a grassy flat where the Jones Hill road emerged from Limekiln Gulch, the town site had many natural advantages. All about it were virgin redwoods; through it ran a lively stream in El Arroyo de Los Gatos; it was the junction of roads and changing place for horses after the hard pull over Jones Hill and later over the steep and narrow turnpike out of Forbes' Mill.

In order to prevent travelers from going free over the old road to and from the Valley, a toll-house was situated about where the bridge at Lexington now (1934) stands on the present highway. Especially for horsemen was the toll gate provided, as most of the heavy traffic preferred the turnpike to the climb over Jones Hill, but riders found little difficulty in negotiating the old route. This toll-house and gate were superseded by a toll station at the edge of Los Gatos in later years.

The importance of the community is indicated in the Pacific Coast Business directory for 1867 which lists the following establishments: George N. Adams, manufacturer of redwood pipe used in the mines at Almaden and Guadalupe; S. H. and J. W. Chase, lumber merchants; Elledge and Seanor, blacksmiths; W. S. Hall, wheelwright; J. W. Lyndon, lumber, groceries, etc.; Isaac Paddock, blacksmith, hotel keeper, postmaster; The Santa Clara Petroleum Company.

Eight sawmills are listed in the directory, including two operated by John (Young) McMillan and one each by the Moody brothers, C.

Thomas, E. Froment, William P. Dougherty, Marion Covel and brother, and S. H. and J. W. Chase. All were run by water power except those of the Froments and Moodys which were steam powered.

Although there were no tanneries in Lexington at the time, leather formed an important part of the industrial life of the community, the directory states:

"Owing to the large size, heavy and firm character of the hides of the cattle slaughtered here (Santa Clara Valley), the sole leather manufactured here is superior to that produced in the tanneries of the eastern states. The bark of the peculiar species of oak (*Lithocarpus densifiora*) found along the coast from Monterey Bay to Mendocino, and particularly in the Santa Cruz Mountains, noted for its excess of tannin, is peculiarly adapted to this purpose, and many of these ancient denizens of the soil have been stripped bare to serve this important end.

"To such an extent has this been carried on in some instances that even the ancient oak upon which the venerated Padre Junipero Serra and his followers commemorated the landing of the first white men upon these shores at the Bay of Monterey, by cutting a large cross deep into the trunk, has been entirely denuded of its bark by some vandal whose bump of reverence for the past has been similarly razed by the utilitarian spirit of the present.

"The largest tanneries of the state, on account of the peculiar advantages afforded by that region, are located in Santa Cruz County," the directory concludes. For many years, however, long lines of pack mules loaded with slabs of tan bark were a common sight in Lexington and elsewhere on the Santa Clara side of the Summit ridge.

Lexington was named by one John Logan, who moved there with his family from Lexington, Kentucky, according to the recollections of George H. McMurtry, city treasurer of Los Gatos, who was born in Lexington in 1865. A conflicting account has it that the place was named by J. P. Henning, one of the two who bought out Buffalo Jones, and who is credited with having laid out the town in 1860. Henning came from Lexington, Missouri. At any rate, it seems to have been named for one of the many Lexingtons scattered around the United States, certainly no later than 1860.

Among its first families, both in point of historic precedence and in social esteem, were the McMurtrys and the McMillans, who were intermarried. Dr. W. S. Mc Murtry, born in Kentucky in 1818, was a prominent St. Louis physician who saw service in the Mexican War. He followed the Gold Rush to California, did some mining at Grass Valley before moving to Lexington (then Jones' Mill) in the early 1850s.

Before coming to California he married Olive A. McMillan, sister of John Young McMillan, one of the most famous millmen of the region for years to come. McMillan preceded Dr. McMurtry to California in 1852. Shortly after arriving at Jones' Mill he married Parneta Howell, a daughter of Watkins F. Howell of Reservoir Ranch.

The Howells

Watkins Howell, whose prowess as a bear hunter was described earlier, was one of the region's earliest settlers. The story of the Howell family is the typical "covered-wagon" saga of the 1850s—an entire family of "in-laws" starting out together for the new El Dorado.

In the party were Watkins Howell and his wife, Mary; their three small children, Ellen, Parneta and Nancy; Howell's father, James Howell; and Mrs. Howell's parents, Alexander and Sarah Ogan, and their large family of six girls and three boys, mostly grown. The party left Kentucky, Missouri, in 1852. En route to California a baby girl was born to Mrs. Ogan. As the party was then approaching the Sierra Nevada range, the child was named Sierra Nevada Ogan, a true covered-wagon baby.

They arrived in California in the fall of the same year. The Howells stopped at Grass Valley to mine for two years before joining the Ogans who had moved on to Berryessa in the Santa Clara Valley. Like many another settler in the Valley at the time, Ogan had to spend thousands of dollars clearing title to the property he tried to homestead against the multifold claims made against every square foot of Valley land.

After two years at Berryessa, Howell purchased from a man named Shearer (an early homesteader) 320 acres of land at what is now known as the Reservoir Ranch of the San Jose Water Company. Here he moved his growing family, which now included Alexander M. Howell, born at Berryessa June 13, 1854, the first "native son" in the family. Howell planted an orchard and vineyard and spent most of the succeeding years taking out split lumber and tan-bark.

In the early 1860s he drained the upper lagoon (now Howell reservoir) and planted the wonderfully fertile peat lands of the lake bottom in vegetables, fruits, and grapes, for which there was much demand at the nearby sawmills and at the Almaden and Guadalupe mines. With his extensive ranch holdings and an increasing family he was kept on the run until 1876, when he sold the reservoir site to the San Jose Water Company for $2000, according to his son, J. Frank Howell of San Jose. The following year his daughter, Emma, died at the age of nineteen, first of the family to go.

In 1879 Howell sold the rest of the ranch to one Frank Baker and moved to Los Gatos, where he and his family lived until 1883, when they moved to Washington state, near where the Scott Hall and Elledge families, Lexington pioneers, had previously settled. Their family now included Parneta, Nancy, Alexander, Emma Frances, James F., Charles W., Sarah, and John Martin Howell, and Ellen Belcher, daughter of Mrs. Howell by a previous marriage, who married Josiah Chase, noted millman.

Housekeepers were much in demand in those days, and women could well afford to pick and choose as they were in the minority in a world of men. Four of the Ogan daughters, grown when they arrived in Berryessa, were soon carried to the altar. One of them, Josie, came to Lexington to visit her sister, Mrs. Howell, and met and married Charles Paddock, brother of the Lexington hotel owner.

But all was not happy with the Howells and Ogans. Stark tragedy struck suddenly in 1854 when Elizabeth Ogan, who had married a man named Willis, was stabbed to death by a bandit on the doorstep of her home. In 1891 Mrs. Howell was critically injured in a train wreck en route from Portland to California, and never fully recovered. She died in Washington state in 1894 and was buried there beside her son, John, who preceded her in death in 1887. Her husband died June 2, 1896, also in Washington state.

A Famous Murder Case

The Howell family was not the only one which tragedy stalked in those early days of violence—it was only a mile or two from Lexington that William P. Renowden and Archie McIntyre were horribly murdered in a crime that has come down to the present day as the "McIntyre-Renowden" murder. The account of the deed is contained at great length in the *San Jose Mercury* starting Tuesday morning, March 13, 1883, two days after the crime, and occupying columns of space every day thereafter for months.

Flames from their little mountain cabin on the old Dougherty mill road attracted several residents of the region to the scene early Tuesday morning. Renowden, shot full of holes and partly burned, was found near the smoking remains of the cabin. Within the ruins of the cabin the charred body of his partner, Archie McIntyre, was discovered. He, too, had been shot. Woodsmen who were well liked throughout the mountains, the two men were widely known, and their death shocked the entire county. An investigation was launched at once.

At the coroner's inquest the following morning, L. L. Majors, a saloon keeper of ill-repute, implicated Joseph Jewell, itinerant painter, and John Showers, rancher, giving damaging testimony against both. Showers disappeared in the hue and cry that at once arose, but was captured by Deputy Sheriff George E. Bennett of Gilroy the next Monday evening. When the inquest was resumed the following day Showers promptly made a full confession, naming Majors as instigator of the plot.

According to Showers, he and Jewell went to the Renowden cabin at Majors' suggestion, declaring that Majors had armed them with a pistol and gave them a pair of pliers with which to "pull out the old man's finger-nails to make him talk." Renowden was reputed at that time to have had large sums of money hidden about the place. But the plan, carefully worked out, failed to operate on schedule, and in the middle of the battle that arose, the two men killed McIntyre and Renowden. Returning to Los Gatos they told their story to Majors, who gave them a flask of whiskey and $5 and told them to "flee for their lives."

The story was substantiated in detail the following day when the inquest was resumed, this time at the court house in San Jose, when Showers made his formal confession in full. Majors refused to testify at the time, having no attorney, and was excused.

The verdict of the coroner's jury was reported as finding that McIntyre and Renowden had met their deaths from pistol shots inflicted by Joseph Jewell, and that said Jewell was assisted by one John Showers, and aided, and encouraged by L. L. Majors, and afterward assisted by said L. L. Majors to escape. Majors was described in following accounts as "an attorney, blacksmith, carpenter and carriage maker, an active member of the church (in San Jose) and temperance worker, a member of the Grand Army post and of the Los Gatos lodge of A.O.U.W."

Early Monday morning, March 20, word was received of the capture of Joseph Jewell at Fresno, whence he was returned by Sheriff Branham. Met at the jail by a huge mob, Jewell was rushed into a cell only after a show of arms by the sheriff. Arraigned before Justice Vance the afternoon of March 20, all three pleaded not guilty.

Meanwhile, a small mob of curiosity seekers continued to gather at the jail and indignation ran unstayed in Los Gatos, where Majors' saloon was wrecked. A cellar under the saloon was excavated in the belief that the body of at least one murdered man thought to have been killed by Majors would be found, but nothing was turned up. Attorneys were advised by the crowd that it would be "unprofitable" to undertake the defense of any of the three.

A brief account appearing the *Mercury* March 25, described visits at the jail of 2,500 people: "Majors was gloomy as usual and applied himself closely to reading a Bible, while Showers seemed as proud as a corporal with his first stripes. Jewell maintained a cheerful appearance all day, although he was apparently very nervous."

A ring-around-the-rosy started the proceedings Monday morning, March 26, with the court jammed to overflowing with spectators, while W. B. Hardy, attorney for L. L. Majors, demanded a private hearing. Jewell and Showers were still without counsel. Started behind closed doors late in the afternoon, the hearing was resumed the following morning. At that time, five newspapermen appeared as counselors designated by John Showers, thwarting a move of Majors' counsel to exclude the press from the hearing.

Showers' testimony occupied the entire hearing of Tuesday, but the following day Hardy succeeded in having the press excluded from the hearing, bringing wrathful comment from the *Mercury;* however, a telephone concealed in the dome of the courtroom disclosed the entire proceedings to the indefatigable reporters of the day, and full accounts duly appeared in the papers as usual. "Grapevine" telephone and reporters armed with opera glasses reported the next day's proceedings in equally full style, together with pungent comments on the apoplectic wrath of Hardy, Majors' counsel, at his inability to muzzle the press.

After a prolonged trial, Joseph Jewell was found guilty of murder in the first degree on Friday, May 11, and time of sentence was set for two weeks hence. Meanwhile preparations of Majors' trial, postponed because of the delay in trying Jewell, were opened. Majors' trial started Saturday morning, May 12, and was made more exciting in the midst of it by a full and damning confession by Jewell, definitely implicating Majors. On Sunday morning, May 27, the jury brought in a verdict of murder in the first degree, with life imprisonment.

On Saturday, June 3, Jewell was sentenced to death on the gallows, while Showers and Majors were formally committed to the penitentiary for life by Judge Belden. The day for execution, July 27, was postponed until November 30, by Governor George Stoneman on a petition for reprieve, despite furious comment from all sides that filled the papers for weeks.

As a final windup of the affair, which heaped notoriety on the county not surpassed until the present day, Jewell was hung at San Quentin on November 30, 1883; Showers was stabbed to death in a prison row some time later; and L. L. Majors met his death in a prison break at Folsom several years afterward, one of the wildest escapades in the annals of crime.

Stagecoaches and Socials

Even in the tragedy and strife of those early days Lexington continued to grow for a time. Isaac Paddock erected a large hotel and stage station where the six-horse stages between San Jose and Santa Cruz stopped. His wife, Sarah, carried on the business after Paddock's death. George Colgrove, stage coach driver and operator of later railroad fame, at one time operated two stage barns here also.

Profiting from the stage runs and the many teams that ran through the village, wheelwright Scott Hall did a flourishing business in conjunction with his son-in-law, William H. Elledge, a blacksmith who had built a home here for his bride, Pay Hall, in 1856. Elledge moved to Washington state in 1870 and died there. Mrs. Elledge survived until 1923.

Lexington was also the social center of the mountain region prior to the 1880s and the scene of many an old-time dance attended by ranchers and woodsmen from far and wide.

That there was little love lost in that period between the mountain people and those of the Valley, an amusing incident of 1864 reveals. Ten couples left Lexington one night to attend a dance in Santa Clara, where they were greeted with the appellation of "redwood splinters." Hearing this, Bill Elledge, the young and brawny blacksmith who was one of the party, stepped out on the floor and offered to demonstrate that he and his pals were more like saw-logs than splinters, if anyone cared to step a few rounds with them. No one did, and the incident passed peacefully.

With the arrival of the railroad in Los Gatos it became apparent that Lexington was to suffer and the first families moved away. Soon the Halls, Elledges, McMurtrys, Howells, and others were gone. Stages no longer stopped at Lexington but operated from Los Gatos at the Ten Mile House (later Hotel Lyndon) until the tunnels were completed.

As the village waned, Los Gatos grew. Martin Covel, who bought stumpage (uncut timber) from Howell and made enough money to build a sawmill in the upper canyon, later purchased the Ten Mile House and the land where the Southern Pacific depot now (1934) stands—it was a hayfield then. But Covel went into the red on the deal and sold out to John Lyndon, another early-day Lexington resident, who moved the hotel across the street in 1877 to make room for the railroad station.

The History of Alma

While Lexington was in the midst of its vigorous, boisterous adolescence, a quieter but nonetheless significant community was springing up a mile to the south.

Here was the Forest House, a stage station and hostelry destined to become the post office of Alma twenty years later, a half-dozen mills, and a store. Here was the schoolhouse erected by Louis Hebard, where the mountain children from Lexington, the Howell family, and others as far away as the Summit region could eke out a few months of book learning each year.

Where the Jesuit order is now (1934) engaged in remodeling the old redwood residence on the Tevis estate, near the site of a home built in the 1890s by James L. Flood, James Howe had erected a mill in the middle 1850s. He dammed a lagoon, piped water in from Webb creek, and operated an overshot waterwheel which in turn powered an up-and-down "muley" saw.

(The operator of the saw, incidentally, slept while the painfully slow sawing process went on, and then awoke when the sawed board dropped to the floor and the log was ready for another run. The process was not much faster than the whip-sawing method it replaced, but it was a lot less work for the sawyers—especially the one down in the pit—and was much in vogue before the advent of the circular saw.)

Webb creek, which supplied water for the wheel, was named after an early-day mill operator whose mill occupied almost the exact spot where the Flood home later was built, not far from the Howe mill and lagoon.

Into the mountains in the early 1860s to work for Howe came Lysander Collins, who had arrived the year before in Alviso from Pennsylvania with his wife, Elisa Taylor, and their small son, Joseph. While Mrs. Collins and the boy lived in Calavcras Valley with relatives,

Collins, a former raftsman on the Susquehanna and a skilled lumberman, worked that first summer for his wages in the woods.

Collins acquired land on the old stage road by the simple process of occupying it, took timber from the Howe mill in lieu of wages, and in 1862 built a home for himself and his family, including a saloon, hotel, and dining room for a stage station.

This home, the first Forest House, and the first important structure in the village of Alma-to-be, stood on the south side of Collins Creek at the junction of the present Santa Cruz Highway with the Aldercroft road to Wright's. It was an imposing two-story structure for those days in the mountains, with its four upstairs bedrooms, and saloon, dining room, kitchen, and more bedrooms on the ground floor.

To insure his precarious land titles at this stage, Collins purchased from Howe and Howe's son-in-law, William Weldon, two 100-acre tracts under school land warrants which later proved worthless. Included in the deal was the old Howe farmhouse on a knoll nearby, into which the family moved a short while after a storm arose one night in 1865, flooded Collins Creek behind a log jam about where the highway now runs, and swept through the Forest House. For a short time the family camped in what was left of the saloon while the torrent raged through the kitchen and dining rooms, which were thus provided with running water decades before piped plumbing reached the mountains. From there they moved to the Howe house.

Meanwhile one E. Froment, a French millman who was engaged in logging in the Logan & Whitehurst gulch, was running his logs down a two-mile tramway to a mill located on the north side of Collins Creek, on the very spot where the state forestry fire station was built in the 1930s. (An old wooden wheel unearthed by workmen at the station and deposited in the museum at the Montezuma school bears testimony to the mill location, on land acquired by Collins.)

Froment vacated the place after he had been cutting for two years, and the property was promptly "jumped" by one G. K. White, moving apparently at the instigation of a man named Younger, a Santa Clara real estate operator. While Collins went into court to reclaim his land, White and Younger enterprisingly built a new and still more imposing

Lysander Collins's Forest House south of Alma, c. 1870. A stage company "mud wagon," used in bad weather, stands in front.

Forest House on the old mill site, with six rooms below and ten above—the largest hostelry between Los Gatos and Santa Cruz.

The school land warrants were valueless the court decided, and it finally took an act of Congress to confirm the titles. Congress decreed that all who had settled in good faith under school warrant titles could assume homestead and preemption rights dating back to the warrant dates, thus restoring the land to Collins, who found himself in possession of a new, larger and better Forest House for nothing more than his court costs.

Another less protracted land dispute was settled out of court when Collins took the law into his own hands. In running his fence line along the creek, Collins discovered that a portion of the Webb home, later occupied by the James Newell family, projected into his property. An argument arose, and when Collins went armed with a rifle to run the fence, house or no house, he found the Webb tribe out in force with shotguns to block his path. But in the show of arms, the Webbs backed down and Collins hacked a hole right through the back of the Webb house to complete his fence line.

It was along about this time that the village stopped being called Forest House and became Alma by edict of the U.S. Post Office Department. On the same trip that he named the post office at Fowler's Summit "Patchen," a postal inspector decided to call the Forest House "Alma," which is Spanish for "soul" and means nothing whatever in connection with the location, its history, its families, or anything else.

Apparently he picked the name at random because Forest House, in his mind, sounded too much like Forest Grove, Oregon. This was in 1873, when the post office was finally established with Lysander Collins as first postmaster.

(Author's note—The post office continued in operation until 1952, when the town was abandoned to make way for Lexington reservoir which now covers both Alma and Lexington.)

As Alma prospered, Lexington suffered, for it was the Lexington post office that was moved to the Forest House from its former location for a variety of reasons. One was the flood of complaints that came from church people of the mountains who did not like having their women and children passing through the saloon at Lexington to reach the post office in the rear.

In addition to mail service, carried by stagecoach along with a Wells Fargo contract, Alma enjoyed local express service daily to and from San Jose provided by Ben Fessenden, who lived just west of Steven Chase's grocery store.

The store principally supplied the large Chase and Connolly mill in the gulch above the Howell reservoir on Chase Road, but it was also patronized by many mountain families. Food supplies did not offer much of a problem since venison hunters, honey gatherers, and fishermen traveled the roads daily. Huge trout were to be had in most of the streams (which in those days ran unimpeded to the sea) and were peddled by commercial Isaac Waltons all over the mountains.

Trout Gulch

From this custom of peddling fish arose one of the most humorous of mountain legends—one that carries over to this day whenever a gullible visitor meets one of the many mountain jokesters.

The story has to do with Trout Gulch, an intermittent mountain torrent that cuts down the west side of the canyon near Lexington. Countless fishermen have been directed to this sometimes stream by natives who point out that it was named "Trout creek" for its supply of innumerable, stupendous trout.

Trout Gulch, however, was not named for the fish, directly, and it never did contain anything larger than a minnow. It is far too steep, and dry between storms, to support a real fish colony. It was named for an odd character, a Greek fish peddler who lived with his Indian "wife" somewhere in back of Lexington in the 1850s. This Greek spoke no English and his name was unpronounceable by the local citizens, but he did know the word "trout," which he mistook to apply to all kinds of fish. So he became known as "Trout," as did the little creek where he lived.

Oddly enough, he never peddled trout, but fish from the sea. He and his mule made frequent trips to Santa Cruz, where he bought a quantity and variety of fish—bass, sole, cod, and the like—which he peddled through the hills crying "Trout ! Trout!" without the slightest regard to the species that happened to be in his basket at the time. But he sold the fish, which was the main thing, and probably was just as happy as the succeeding generations of pranksters have been with their citified victims.

Grizzly Stories

Popular from the beginning as a stage stop and watering place for men and horses alike (the one in the saloon, the other in the trough), Forest House was famous for its fare, especially with the stage passengers from elsewhere. A great desire to taste the meat of the almost fabulous grizzly bears that roamed the hills in the early days possessed those tourists, although in fact the meat was tough, stringy, and almost unpalatable. The mountain people would not touch the stuff and said it tasted like rancid fish. To supply this novel demand, inasmuch as grizzly bears were already becoming scarce when Forest House started, was the duty of a hunter of no mean accomplishments in that line—one Thomas Damien, who lived at White Rock, near the head of Bear Creek on the other side of the mountain.

In his frequent trips down to Lexington and Alma, following the old trail from Brown's summit and down the Dougherty mill road, Damien nearly always brought with him a big chuck of fresh bear meat, which promptly appeared on the menu for the edification of the unwary.

Dougherty mill, which gave its name to the road now called Bear Creek Road on both sides of the ridge, was located on either of two of the smaller branches of the upper Zayante. Its output, however, was hauled over the top of the mountain to the finishing mills at Lexington and Alma, a considerable feat in itself.

Across the canyon, in the region still known as Hooker Gulch, was the mill of John Young McMillan, previously mentioned at some length, who employed one Billy Hooker. Billy had little to do with the gulch except that he lived in a cabin beside it, and spent his days patching up McMillan's skid roads. Billy's name, however, is perpetuated on government maps, while MacMillan (sometimes spelled McMillin) is without a namesake in the entire region he so greatly aided in development.

Gulches, it seems, were nearly always named for people who lived on or in them—first or last. What is now known as Soda Spring Canyon was in the 1860s known as Conoyer Gulch. Conoyer, who camped on the flat at the mouth of the Canyon, manufactured excellent smoking pipes out of hard manzanita root, very similar to the famous French briar, and sold them all over the mountains.

He obtained the root from a dense grove at the head of the creek. On one occasion he failed to show up over night, and the next day friends started searching for him armed to the teeth against bears. After a while a shout caught their attention. "Look o-o-o u t! It's a bear!" Conoyer yelled. It was Conoyer up a tree where he had spent the night with a large she-grizzly tearing up the turf around its base. (Unlike other bears, grizzlies do not climb trees.) The bear ran away as the armed party approached.

A man named Boyd followed Conoyer to the gulch, and then one John Cavance, grandfather of Hal Chase, the noted baseball player, arrived. Cavance, from Santa Barbara, was a venison-and-honey hunter who sold his harvest to hungry mountaineers. Cavanaugh Gulch is the name still carded on some maps of the region, an odd misspelling of Cavance.

Bear fights were by no means as frequent in the region as the variously decorated legends of the time would indicate, according to Lysander Collins' son Joseph. Despite his nearly eighty years, Collins possesses a phenomenal memory from which much of this account is drawn.

Collins, as mentioned earlier, lived much of his life, from when he was six years old until he was a grown man, at the Forest House, prowled the woods and streams constantly, and never saw a bear! Tracks there were a-plenty, but nary a "bar" for Joe Collins or his son. The big animals kept to the hills pretty well and were ruthlessly hunted down whenever their depredations into livestock sufficiently aroused the ire of the mountain ranchers. The result was that within a short time after the arrival of permanent settlers, bears soon became scarce.

Lysander Collins operated the Forest House until 1878, when he and his wife went back east to visit relatives. Part of his property he sold to a man named Wilcox, superintendent of the San Jose Water Company, who let the irrigation water rights established by Collins lapse, whereupon they fell into the hands of the water company.

Soda Springs

Collins died a few years later, and the balance of his land was inherited by his two sons, Joseph and Hugh. Included in the estate was the much-disputed land at the soda springs above Alma, where years before E. Cavance, an uncle of Hal Chase, had discovered the soda-bearing waters bubbling out of the rocks while on a hunting trip.

A man named Meysenheimer filed preemption rights on what he thought was the spring-bearing property, claiming 360 acres. He sought to develop the springs for medicinal properties, built trails to the scene, and was promptly laughed off the mountain. When Collins bought him out and had the land surveyed, he found that Meysenheimer's claim fell just ten feet short of the mineral springs. In the meantime, Jacob Rich, a San Jose speculator of note, had purchased a half-interest with an eye toward development. Then a couple of Italians filed on the adjoining government land and claimed the springs, and the case went to court where it remained for decades, in suit after suit.

Louis Hebard

Mentioned several times in these pages is Louis Hebard, one of the earliest settlers in the Alma region, who took up 160 acres near the present Idlewild property in 1857. A New York carpenter, Hebard built many of the homes in the region as well as the Lexington school house when it stood near the Forest House. Coming here with the Gold Rush, he entered the mountains to work in several of the mills around Lexington, including those of Howe & McMillan, Froment, Whitehurst, Rickets, and others.

His first house was built of split lumber with a puncheon floor, but he added sawed-lumber additions to transform the little square shack into a respectable-sized home that stood until about 1932.

In 1875 he married Lodiska Ann Girard, widow of Artemius Wallace Murdock, who had died three years earlier at Patchen. Mrs. Murdock was the mother of Charles W.C. Murdock, who is now (1934) living near the old home-place after an absence of more than thirty years.

A small boy when he first came here with his mother, Murdock well remembers early-day incidents recounted by his step-father, including reminiscences about Buffalo Jones who pointed out to Hebard the spot where Frémont camped in 1846.

It was on this spot, near the Hebard homestead, that Murdock claims that he (not Hebard) found the remains of an old army saddle and a rusty cavalry spur believed to have been left by Frémont's party. An open, grassy flat now grown over with brush was the scene of the encampment, now on Idlewild property. The stumps of huge redwoods tell the story of the lumbering activity that went on in the 1850s.

The Tevis Estate at Alma

Scarcely deserving the name "ghost town" because of the current (1934) activity centered about it, Alma boasts among its proudest possessions the wide expanse of the Tevis estate, formerly owned by the late James L. Flood and now owned by the Jesuit order.

To the old-timers of the region the place was known as the "Knowles ranch," and earlier still as the "Fish ranch," the latter designation doubtless arising from the excellent trout to be found in its streams and natural ponds.

Sweeping up from Los Gatos Creek to the crest of Castle Rock ridge back of the town, in a well-watered, beautifully timbered swale, the place was well-settled long before any of the names listed were applied.

First to appreciate its possibilities as an extensive estate, however, was Captain Stillman H. Knowles, the famous Captain Harry Knowles of the San Francisco vigilantes fame in 1856 and a millionaire mining associate of James Clair Flood, the Bonanza King of the Comstock Lode. Knowles made his stake in Oregon at the famous old E. & E. mine at Baker City. He returned to California, bought up forty-nine acres at Alma from Wilbur Wilcox, acquired water rights from Ben Rankin, and prepared to reproduce here his ideal, a remembrance carried from boyhood of his grandfather's home in New England.

He erected a large and picturesque home, and clearing away a number of tule ponds in his "front yard" converted them into ten trout lakes, in which he propagated splendid rainbow trout with the intention of building up a commercial fish farm.

The idea was not new—the region was noted for its native trout, and others had thought of commercial trout-raising without doing much about it, although Ben Rankin a decade before had attempted to raise German carp, then a sporting game fish, up on top of the ridge. But the plan did not go over for some reason, and Captain Knowles finally gave it up and sold out to James L. Flood, son of the Bonanza King, in 1894. Knowles died three years later, leaving behind many anecdotes about his vigorous activity.

One of Captain Harry' s chief delights was in road racing with his apparently ancient and decrepit nag, "Old Bill," a large white horse on whose hip bones a straw hat could be hung with ease. With Bill hitched to a light cart, Knowles would amble leisurely down the road until some gay young blade in a shining new dogcart, out with his best gift, attempted to pass in a swift of dust. Then Captain Harry would give Old Bill a touch of the whip, the big horse would unlimber his ungainly joints, and soon the young blade would be wondering if his horse had been hitched to a tree.

Such is one of the many stories told of Captain Harry and Old Bill—mountain legends now more indicative of the spirit of the time and the man than of the veracity of the accounts in their present form.

A wide circle of acquaintances flocked to the ranch during the brief stay of Captain Knowles, including many famous characters in San Francisco history. His daughter, Miss Frances M. Knowles, who died early in 1934, inherited most of his estate, but lost her fortune in Goldfield, Nevada, when the mining boom there collapsed. She was an inveterate greyhound racing fan and was known as one of the organizers of the sport in California.

In a blaze of glory which accompanied his lavish expenditures, James L. Flood arrived on the scene as Knowles departed, buying up large blocks of land from the small ranches all around, acquiring title to some of the larger holdings of Louis Hebard, the San Jose Water Company, the Minnis family, the Sheffers, the Rundells, John O' Day, and others, until his holdings ran into the hundreds of acres.

From a contemporary account may be obtained an excellent picture of the estate as it then appeared, when Flood began pouring into the place the benefit of his millions in an apparent effort to reproduce at Alma "a wee bit o' heaven":

Paradise and Perfect Rest
(from the *San Francisco Chronicle*
November 3, 1895)

"James L. Flood is transforming a bit of the Santa Cruz Mountains into a paradise for his wife and a perfect resting place for himself.

"In July of 1894 Mr. Flood, to gratify his wife, bought Alma Dale, a pretty place of 50 acres. S. H. Knowles had owned it for seven years and had done much to make it attractive. The Dale included the most commanding points of observation in a big pocket of the mountains along the South Pacific Coast railway north from Alma station. Knowles had built a roomy house and a barn for 15 horses, besides planting a choice vineyard and an orchard in which was everything from olives to apples.

"A strong mountain brook traversed the tract, and every available site held a dam and a pond behind it—nine ponds in all—and into each a good supply of rainbow trout was turned...

"When Mr. Flood began his work he found the original tract too small and at once set about adding to it, until at present he owns more than 800 acres, including the whole watershed of the Alma brook as well as a number of springs. An ample supply of pure water is carried by gravity to the grounds near the residence.

"The Knowles residence has been reconstructed into a handsome villa of 40 rooms, with a broad veranda and every luxurious fitting that San Francisco decorators and furnishers could provide. The house stands on a shoulder of the mountain two miles above Alma, a site from which a fair sweep of many miles of forest, canyons, rocks, and purple deer brush can be enjoyed in all the varying lights.

"In revamping the place, Mr. Flood's attention was first given to modernizing the stables. All the unemployed carpenters about Los Gatos were hired, together with gardeners and laborers, a merry force of about twenty men who were carried to and from their work in a four-in-hand each day.

"In place of Knowles' big old-fashioned barn, there is now a structure that cost $15,000. Flooring, stalls and the finish of the stables are polished in native wood. There are brasses in profusion, much glass, rooms for harness, whips, robes, and the dozen or more vehicles now in use.

"Water piped under high pressure is everywhere about the place, and throughout are labor-saving devices which enable a small force of grooms to care for the 25 animals now in use.

"Besides a stud of saddle horses, Mr. Flood has teams for carriage use, others for the road wagons and carts in which most of mountain driving is done. Then there are heavy draft horses for the work of the place. . . .

"The soil of the Flood preserve is rich and warm and will produce in perfection all the fruits and nuts which can be grown in the most favored parts of California. Flowers grow riotously, and besides the freer sorts the tract flourishes with native blooms of many colors and shades. . . .

"But to the owner, the glory of the place is in its rare offering in the way of sport. At his door is a lake, seven acres in area, fringed with willows and azaleas. It is as placid as a mountain sky, except when a grasshopper or midge is blown into the pool. Then a dozen busy trout break the calm for the morsel.

"The former owner of the Dale was an enthusiast as to trout and stocked the waters with the rainbow fish common to California streams. There are now to be native trout in one lake, eastern trout in another, bass in a third, and such additional game fish as may seem likely to thrive. . . .

"He is to introduce pheasants and brown quail, there being much land just suited to these birds. Besides the quail and the trout, the Flood tract is well stocked with deer, which will rapidly increase under proper protection . . . it will be possible to enjoy the finest of hunting and still have good venison without affecting the supply.

"The Bear Creek county road passes the Flood mansion, but in common with the roads of the locality, is rough and dusty. To avoid both discomforts, Flood is building a private carriageway from the home over his own property all the way to Alma. . . .

"A low estimate of the expenditures involved in the place is at least $250,000. Mr. Flood gave employment to the mechanics of the neighborhood by preference, and the weekly payment of wages to them during the 15 months of their labor having gone far toward preventing privation in Los Gatos. . . ."

Incidentally, although James L. Flood, owner of the estate, was frequently referred to in the press as the "Bonanza King," it was his father, James Clair Flood, who established the family fortune and is entitled to the royal appellation.

James Clair Flood, a San Francisco saloon keeper, born on Staten Island, New York, in 1826, received only a limited education before he left for California in 1849 to join the Gold Rush. It was in Nevada that he made his big strike, forming, along with James G. Fair, John W. Mackay and William S. O'Brien, the "Big Four" who opened the great Comstock lode and later discovered what was to become the famous Consolidated Virginia mine, at one time reputed to be worth $160,000,000. Flood died in Germany in 1889. This was the fortune which fell into the laps of James L. Flood and his sister, Cora. James died in 1926, leaving an estate of some $18,500,000, still a considerable sum.

Early in 1906, Alma Dale passed into the hands of Dr. Harry L. Tevis, retired San Francisco physician, who resided at Alma the last twenty-five years of his life, adding to the land holdings until they totaled 2,500 acres and adding new buildings.

A permanent staff of from twenty-five to one hundred servants and ranch hands aided him in the maintenance of a huge experimental farm, renowned dahlia and rose gardens, and extensive stables where he made a study of horse breeding. Soon after he purchased the estate it was brought to the public eye when Dr. Tevis opened his doors to an entire grand opera company, refugees from the San Francisco earthquake and fire.

Dr. Tevis died July 19, 1931, in San Francisco, leaving an estate valued at $5,818,700, one of the largest ever probated in the Santa Clara County courts. He distributed the estate among his few surviving relatives, friends, employees, and charitable institutions. His ashes were scattered over the highest point on the ranch, in accordance with a dying request.

His palatial home, gardens and equipment were estimated to have cost in the neighborhood of $750,000, including a magnificent library of 7,000 volumes, extensive acreage in rare flowers, and a private water system ample for a small city.

Formerly famous up and down the state for its horses, the estate had largely been forgotten by the public until the opening of the Constance May Gavin case in 1926. Well remembered by Alma residents, some of whom appeared as witnesses in the case, Mrs. Gavin played as a girl at Alma Dale, where she was commonly believed to be an adopted daughter of Flood. She, however, claimed that he was her father. The suit was settled out of court in Redwood City for $1,200,000.

Last April (1934) a major portion of the property was sold to the Sacred Heart Novitiate of Los Gatos and the Jesuit order, to be transformed into a theological college with vineyards to be planted on a large part of the land.

At present thirty acres have been cleared for grapes, and an additional thirty acres will be similarly treated this fall. The main residence has been converted into an administration building for the novitiate, while a large 52-room dormitory is being erected nearby in the Swiss chalet style of the residence. Dr. Tevis's library is being remodeled for a chapel.

The Largest Madrone

Thirty lumber mills operated for seventy years on the eastern slopes of the Santa Cruz Mountains above Los Gatos, changing the landscape from a verdant parkland of giant redwoods to dense, chaparral-covered slopes with rocky gullies carved by erosion in many areas. What the timber crews missed, raging forest fires that swept the mountains at intervals completed in destruction, leaving only a few remnants of what had once been the most heavily timbered redwood region south of Humboldt County.

Here and there, however, is to be found a lone relic, like the gigantic redwood known as the Mt. Charley tree (described in an earlier chapter), or the lesser known madrone giant on the Tevis ranch, later Alma College of the Jesuit Order, just above Alma.

(Author's note—This tree fell sometime in the 1950s, the exact date not being a matter of record.)

This magnificent madrone once stood on the Tevis estate near
Alma.

It so greatly exceeds in dimension any other member of its species
in these mountains, there would seem to be little doubt as to the
authenticity of its claim to be the world's largest madrone. A mighty
tree of its kind when Captain John C. Frémont passed it in 1846, it is
still today a breath-taking sight, reminiscent of a day when it was but
one of an apparently endless forest of madrones, filling the glades where
redwoods had failed to take a stand.

Spreading a canopy close to 100 feet across, the tree measures 32
feet, 10 inches at its 'waist'—the narrowest portion of the trunk above
the swelling roots and below the first fork eight feet up. Perfectly sym-
metrical in shape, over 10 feet in diameter, the tree branches into two
main trunks, either of which would put to shame almost any other
madrone in the Santa Cruz Mountains.

"The world's largest madrone," on the Tevis estate, c. 1934.

The tree stands in plain sight from Bear Creek Road, just back of the horse barns below the main house on the old Tevis ranch, but because of its immense size and shape it appears at a distance to be an oak even to a careful observer.

A botanically inclined professor once came from Los Angeles to view the tree at the request of his friend, Dr. Harry Tevis. The professor was skeptical, having a pet madrone of his own down by Santa Barbara he regarded as the world's largest, but a glance at this specimen, plus some measurements with a steel tape, soon dispelled any lingering trace of Southern California loyalty, and the honors went to Alma.

Old Graveyards

Less aged, less impressive than the great madrone for their size and grandeur, but nonetheless reminiscent of the days of departed glory in the mountain region are the hidden cemeteries, forgotten and forlorn, that stand near Alma—one within a mile of the madrone.

In them may be found the whole picture of the lives and the tragedies of the pioneer settlers. Death in childbirth, in illness and in violence are recorded on the picturesque headstones that still stand, with their curious sentiments and crude verses that represented a last attempt to pay homage to one loved and grieved.

Graveyards are to be found all through the mountain region, wherever death occurred in mid-winter when storm-bound roads prevented transportation to formal grounds, when services were brief and often without clerical assistance. Where one member of a family was buried, another would follow, until the custom was established and another burial ground instituted beneath a secluded grove.

Such is the Rundell cemetery, the one nearest the big madrone, so named because to be found in it are the graves of many of the Rundell family and their neighbors—early settlers in the Bear Creek Road (Dougherty Mill Road) region above Lexington and Alma.

Few of the stones actually are still standing, all bear the marks of the vicissitudes of time and weather, overgrown with ivy, while tangled poison oak, scrub oak, madrone, and gloomy cypress spring from the graves themselves.

Here is the grave of Isaac Paddack (1827–1873) one-time hotel keeper at Lexington. (His name is spelled Paddock everywhere but on his gravestone). Here are the graves of John Cavance (spelled Cavanaugh), of the gulch beating his misspelled name, and his wife, Eliza, and of others less known now.

Of the fifty graves in the plot, less than half a dozen are now (1934) marked and recognizable, although wooden headpieces, their lettering completely obliterated, lie half-concealed in the intruding bush. The graves of Joseph Foster (1822–1902) and Eliza Foster (1819–1908), and Mary E., wife of William A. Bayne, can be identified.

Not far away across canyons, on the property, near Idlewild Inn, is the Hebard cemetery, partly buried in a slide that followed the 1906 earthquake, another plot of fifty graves now almost entirely lost. Like the Rundell cemetery, the place took its name from the family buried there—part of the family of Louis Hebard, pioneer of the Alma region.

The little flat had been the playground of Hebard's daughter who died when she was but four from diphtheria. She was followed by her brother, Francis, age two; by Bert Hebard, who shot himself in a hunting accident, and by George Hebard, nineteen, who died of typhoid.

William D. Van Lone, a nephew of Hebard's wife and a member of a well known family on Castle Rock ridge, and others connected with his family are also buried here, but Van Lone's grave is the only one still recognizable, and less than half a dozen in the plot are still marked. Rats' nests desecrate those carefully fenced; trees occupy the entire space of some of the tragic children's graves; others are buried beneath half a hillside. Stones remain standing over the graves of "M. Eliza, wife of W. W. Dull, died 1883; Jemima A., wife of E. H. Evans, died November 18, 1862, aged eighteen years," and "Charlotte, wife of E. Armour, died January 3, 1887."

The Mayor of Alma

All recollections of the region are not tragic, however. Comedy at its best was to be found in the 1890s when Gabriel Beal, self-styled mayor, prophet and news gatherer for Alma, came to town.

Beal wrote for the *Los Gatos Mail* under that name; wrote out-landish stories, homey little personal items and matter-of-fact accident yarns all in the same column and all under the same nom-de-plume. Any resemblance between his writings and the truth must have been purely coincidental.

Where Alma at the time consisted of a store, a blacksmith shop, a hotel, and two saloons, Beal nonchalantly organized an imaginary incorporated city that would have done credit to a metropolis.

He elected himself mayor in his stories, and other well-known residents of the area he named to a variety of non-existent civic offices.

A comprehensive program of street paving, schools and other public buildings, an exhibit for the world' s fair at Chicago, and all the appurtenances of a thriving city were thus given to Alma at the stroke of a pen, much to the amusement of the residents of Los Gatos and neighboring towns, to whom Alma was but a wide place one went through en route to someplace else.

Gabriel Beal died July 14, 1934. In real life he was William Nat Friend, former postmaster of Oakland and one of the best known political figures of his time in the East Bay region. Born in 1870, Nat Friend, as he was commonly known, was an honor student at the University of California where he became president of the student body. He studied for the bar while living above Alma on Soda Springs Road, and was admitted to practice in 1898, at the age of twenty-eight.

In 1906 he was ordained to the ministry, but in 1913 again changed his vocation to that of an undertaker. Under the Coolidge administration he became postmaster of Oakland in 1928. At the time of his death he was president of the Albert Brown company in Oakland.

Alma's Mile of Saloons

Booming for a time in the spectacular summer trade that flourished in the mountains after the coming of the railroad in the last two decades of the century, Alma became a popular picnic spot, rivaling at times even Wright's Station and Sunset Park.

A brisk trade was also realized in this period from passing teams, although the heyday of the stagecoach had passed, and the lumber

industry with its accompanying prosperity had waned into insignifi-
cance. Teamsters, hearty men with a great love for the kind of refresh-
ment that in the 1890s was legally unobtainable in Los Gatos because
of a local option law, provided patronage for the notorious "mile of
saloons" that lined the road from Lexington to Alma.

Here in a declining community of half a dozen resident families
were at one time no less than twelve saloons, thicker than filling stations today. But this was not for long; the competition was too heavy,
and most of them soon faded from sight.

The automobile spelled the doom of Alma's prosperity as a summer
resort—it was too close to civilization even for the laborious travel of
those first old high-wheelers and the puffing "one-lunged" motors
which provided a lucrative trade only for mountain ranchers with stout
teams and tackle to yank stalled gas-buggies from mud holes, sand
holes, dust holes, and ruts that neatly engaged transmission housings.

(If a horse and buggy encountered an autoist on the road, the latter
was required to stop if the buggy pilot simply raised a hand. The venturesome autoist was then required by road courtesy to alight and stand
in front of his roaring vehicle to calm the passing horses. Autos also had
to take the outside of the road whenever meeting a horse-drawn con-
veyance, so that if there was not sufficient room to pass, or if the horses
reared in fright, it was the auto that piled into junk at the bottom of the
gulch, never the horse and buggy.)

A far cry from the bustling scene about the Forest House at the
peak of the mill days in the 1860s, Alma was then, as described, a town
of few permanent inhabitants. Stephen Chase's early-day store had
become John Stewart's mercantile establishment. Stewart was succeeded by L. T. Dolder; Dolder by his brother-in-law, Bohme, and
Bohme by his brother-in-law, George Osmer, the present (1934) pro-
prietor who has been there forty years. John Floyd built and operated
the village blacksmith shop, succeeding Davis & Tice of an earlier date,
and was in turn succeeded by Charles Pierce. John Herlinger was a
shoemaker of this time.

A contemporary history of Santa Clara County (1895) lists Alma
as a freight station noted for its agriculture, the flowering chaparral on
the hillsides all around yielding the much-desired, fragrant chaparral

honey. Roads branching from the town, a freight station and post office, summer homes and the soda springs on the eastern side of the canyon are briefly mentioned in this account.

(Author's note—The Alma post office closed in 1952, since the town, like Lexington, was abandoned to make way for the rising waters of the Lexington reservoir.)

Glenwood

Finis. The last chapter has been written in the long and colorful history of Glenwood, the community that became a ghost town because a highway found and followed an easier and faster route. Only a post office open (1934) twice a day when trains pass through, a hotel that is being converted into barracks for an SERA crew, a little school and a house or two still occupied, remain to recall that here was once a prosperous town.

Located on the highway to which it gave its name, the scenic Glenwood Highway from Los Gatos to Santa Cruz, Glenwood was little more than a convenient stopping place for autoists in large numbers after World War I. Ten years earlier, twenty years, thirty years back, before the coming of the automobile started a new era of travel to destroy the summer vacation trade of the resorts, hot springs, and hotels that flourished all over the mountains, Glenwood was famous.

Its splendid hotel, built in the 1890s, was the haunt of millionaires, and its many adjacent resorts enjoyed a lively patronage all summer long. The day of the Sunday traveler had not yet arrived—when people went anywhere, they went to stay a while. There were no concrete highways, no streamlined autos, no palatial auto stages to transport half a city over half a state in half a day.

But even under the influence of modern travel, Glenwood did not fold its tents as did many another mountain town. Its big freight station and railroad depot were still busy; a store and gas station were reaping the benefits of the growing flood of automobile travel past its front door.

Scarcely had the summer trade dwindled before the building of the Glenwood section of the new highway from Los Gatos to Santa Cruz diverted travel from the tortuous old Soquel road and the Mt. Charley Road to bring a flood of travel—and of business—through the heart of the village. In the years that followed the completion of the road in

This concrete bridge on the Glenwood Highway bears the date of its construction, 1915. Photo taken in 1969.

1916 and its pavement in 1919, this symbol of progress which at first had threatened to destroy the town now came to revive it, for a while.

Once more, however, there came a change—progress moved another step, and the automobile trade on which the town had come to depend, was whisked away. Opening of the new Inspiration Point-Scott' s Valley realignment on Labor Day, 1934, sounded the knell of Glenwood, for the new route was placed high up on the ridge south of town and out of sight. Only an occasional automobile or truck passes through Glenwood now—the wide sweeping curves and smooth grades of the new route take the teeming thousands of weekend travelers as well as the daily traffic well away from Glenwood.

(Author's note—Although nothing is left of Glenwood today except a historical marker, portions of the Glenwood Highway are still in use, roughly paralleling the modern freeway, near the Summit. Highway signs mark the turnoffs. The hotel was demolished in 1970.)

Since the opening of the new route the big Glenwood store and adjacent service station are closed. The railroad depot has been closed for more than a year, and the post office clings precariously to all that is left of the village (1934).

The third era has just closed, the era of the tourist stop. The second stage has been mentioned—the time of Glenwood Hotel, of Summer Home Farm, Magnetic Springs, Mount Pleasant Farm and many others served by trains and horses and wagons.

But for the Glenwood scene as it began, out of the shadow of the forest into a boisterous center of logging activities, the fingers of history reach far back into the story of California after the Gold Rush, of the settlement of the central coast area, touching upon names that have since become famous or faded into obscurity.

In the latter class comes the name of David Burns, bear trapper and shingle-mill operator of the 1850s, about whom almost nothing is known except the name. Burns and a man named Randall once cut shingle bolts from the ridge that still bears his name, on the Martin ranch near Inspiration Point. He also had a mill on the road to Laurel, but it has disappeared into the brush, as has all that was left of a bear trap he built near the present Martin home on top of the ridge.

Earlier in the region than Burns, however, were the Parkers and the Bean family. Of the Parkers nothing is known, although a trail bearing their name followed the ridge south of Glenwood to meet El Camino Real on Burns ridge. They appear to have come and gone before any of the permanent settlers. Mountain legend has it that a great animosity arose between Mrs. Parker and Mrs. Bean, possibly over property rights, a bitter dispute that allegedly led to an exchange of rifle fire, fortunately without damage to either party.

Bean Creek, which runs through Summer Home farm, was named for an early rancher, John Bean, who sold out to Charles C. Martin, founder of Glenwood. Twenty years later Martin also bought out Frank Ross, who had homesteaded the abandoned Parker land.

The Martins

So it is that the story of Glenwood is the story of the Martins, starting with Charles C. Martin, who came from way down east at Eastport, Maine, around the Horn and into the lumber business at Lexington, on the other side of the mountain in the late 1840s.

Three years as a teamster found him with a modest stake and an eye injury due to a flick of a misguided bullwhip, a handicap that took him out of the teamster business. In the early 1850s he moved into the region later known as Glenwood and homesteaded lands adjoining those of Mountain Charley McKiernan, and later bought out John Bean so as to increase his holdings. Additional purchases from time to time added to the land also homesteaded by his wife, Hannah Martin, until the total compared favorably to the holdings of McKiernan, Burrell, and other ambitious pioneers of the region.

The Martins' six children were reared in rude cabins built from slabs with puncheon floors—nothing else was available for building material for a long time to come. An experienced millman, Martin worked in many of the numerous mills that dotted the forest from 1860 until the turn of the century—George Anthony's mill on Bean creek, the big plants in Centennial Gulch, Eaton Gulch and Lockhart Gulch and elsewhere that Charles Platt, Elliott Russell, John Eaton, L. G. and Dwight Grover, and others in the logging industry left their mark on the great redwoods.

In 1873 Martin built and operated a store at what was then called Martinsville but soon became Glenwood. Glenwood acquired a post office by that name in 1880, the year the railroad came through the town by means of a tunnel from the town of Laurel, with Martin as postmaster.

(Author's note—In keeping with the historical tradition of the place, Martin's great-granddaughter, Margaret Koch, was the last postmaster when the post office was closed in 1954. That last post office, incidentally, was built of lumber salvaged from a movie set, the scene of Jeanette MacDonald's last picture, *The Sun Comes Up*, staged at Glenwood by Metro-Goldwyn-Mayer in 1948.)

Among his varied activities, Martin also ran a tollgate and stage station on Mountain Charley Road at the point called Station Ranch. Until the coming of the railroad, rough, steep, crooked and dusty wagon roads were Glenwood's only link with the outside world. One short, steep road led directly up the side of the mountain to connect with the stage route along the top of the ridge to the north. Another road climbed out to the south to drop into Laurel, joining the Vine Hill route to the coast and other roads through Laurel to the east and south. These roads, or portions of them, are still in use as mail routes or for access to summer homes.

When the "new" highway was built in 1916, it was a seven-wonder, since it was constructed under a federal subsidy, reinforced with steel to carry heavy military traffic as a defense measure—for fast troop and artillery movements between San Francisco and Monterey Bay. The route had been a hobby of Martin's. He personally made several surveys before one was adopted by the state and finally approved. In appreciation for his effort, Martin's initials and his footprints were set in the wet concrete during the final stages of construction. Martin died at the age of 88, not long after the new concrete highway was finished in 1919.

Legends of Mexican Bandits

No mountain retreat in California would be complete without its Mexican bandit story—either that of Joaquin Murietta or of Tiburcio Vasquez, who must have slept in every cave from the Oregon border to Mexico in order to provide material for the vast number of stories about them.

Vasquez was reputed to be a friend of Sam Thompson, a man of uncertain origin who had a cabin on the Martin ranch. The cabin stood in a little clump of trees behind Martin's big hotel. Behind the trees a hidden trail led up the ridge to connect with other trails going elsewhere. Vasquez was said to make good use of the trails when fleeing from the law, as he usually was.

Except in wet weather, when Vasquez presumably lay low, the sheriff's posse coming from whatever direction could easily be detected at a considerable distance by the huge dust cloud their horses raised on the unpaved roads.

Thompson would then arouse his sleeping friend, who had plenty of time to slip away unnoticed on one of the several trails, being careful not to raise a telltale dust cloud of his own.

As far back as 1812, when this region was still under Spanish rule, the site of Glenwood was reputed to have been the site of a brutal murder—the lynching of a mission priest, one Father Andre Quintana, by a group of renegade Indians. But other accounts place the scene of the murder as the orchard behind the Santa Cruz Mission. In any event, the culprits were eventually caught, but conveniently died of the plague before they could be tried and hanged properly.

Postscript
Where It All Happened

The Santa Cruz Mountains of California, a thickly forested spur of the Coast Range, extend southward from San Francisco to the Santa Clara-Monterey county line at Chittenden Pass, following approximately the San Andreas fault of earthquake fame.

The range is made up of numerous rounded, more or less parallel ridges rising to an elevation of more than 3,000 feet, bounded on the east by lower San Francisco Bay and the Santa Clara Valley, and on the west by the Pacific Ocean.

For all their proximity to San Francisco and the almost continuous metropolis sprawling far south of San Jose, and to the densely populated shores of Monterey Bay, the mountains remain surprisingly wild.

A road that starts from San Francisco as the scenic Skyline Boulevard runs down the crest the length of the range, diminishing as it goes until it is no more than a dirt track at its southern terminus.

One major freeway, Highway 17, crosses the range, from Los Gatos to Santa Cruz, roughly paralleling the now vanished route of a railroad that ran from 1880 to 1940, crossing and recrossing the remains of several earlier highways, which in turn followed old stage routes and Indian trails.

Several lesser roads also cross the range, but in the overall scale of the mountain vastness, they appear to be nothing more than scratches on the terrain, just as the resorts and settlements south of the San Mateo County line seem no more than pinpricks when viewed from the air.

Before the Gold Rush of 1849, this entire range was cloaked in great redwoods, remnants of which are now preserved in numerous state and county parks (the largest is Big Basin State Park). Logging continues to this day, but on nothing like the vast scale of the redwood lumbering industry following the Gold Rush.

The mountainous portion of southwestern Santa Clara County and a small part of adjacent eastern Santa Cruz County form the locale of these stories; along the old railroad and its nearby highways, along the summit of the range (the county line) south to Loma Prieta, highest point at an elevation of 3,806 feet, and a little beyond.

The stories did not include the abandoned quicksilver mines at Almaden and Guadalupe, the only mines of any consequence in the area, which had already been thoroughly documented by other writers. Nor did the series venture over the mountains to the well-settled valley of the San Lorenzo River, north of Santa Cruz. There a string of towns proceeded from lumber camps to resorts to permanent communities without pausing to become ghosts. Their stories, too, have been told and retold.

Thus for all their diversity and more than a century of recorded history, the hamlets of these stories represent only a fragment of the Santa Cruz Mountains, but a vital fragment rich in lore and legend.

Notes for the Expanded Edition

Since the original 1979 publication of my book, *Ghost Towns of the Santa Cruz Mountains*, I have made many trips to those mountains in search of material for additional stories.

Some of those stories were intended for magazine articles, others for inclusion in a second book entitled *Backdoor Wilderness, The Santa Cruz Mountains of California*. A few extracts from that work are presented here because of their close connection with incidents and subjects touched upon in the original *Ghost Towns*.

For example, there were other notable bear fights in the mountains beside the famous attack upon Mountain Charley McKiernan, at least one of which is commemorated in a place name. Bear Gulch in San Mateo County is named for one such episode, in which a rancher named Ryder lost an ear to a grizzly bear in 1850. Severely mauled and left for dead, Ryder was found in time by friends who carried him to a nearby ranch house. There a visiting sailor sewed him up with a needle and thread. Ryder lived to be known the rest of his life as Grizzly Rider.

Also during those later sojourns I was able to tie up some loose ends. In the Watsonville cemetery I found the grave of Silent Charley Parkhurst, stagecoach driver. The headstone tells how this extraordinary character became the first woman ever to vote in the United States, while masquerading as a man, in the general election of 1868.

Carolyn DeVries provided some magnificent photographs of New Almaden in the 1880s and a copy of her syllabus on the subject from the history course she taught at DeAnza College. This material changed my idea that the subject already had been thoroughly covered and produced a new chapter.

Discoveries such as these are tantalizing to a writer. They suggest that undoubtedly there are as many untold stories about the mountains as have appeared in all the books and articles published to date. If I had another 50 years in which to pursue the subject, it would be worth the effort.

John V. Young, 1984

The Woodside Store/Searsville

Sleeping under giant oaks at the junction of Kings Mountain Road and Tripp Road, the old Woodside Store might be inconspicuous save for the fact that it is obviously out of place in a valley devoted to expensive and extensive country estate and suburban homes.

But this slab-sided, one-story structure is a bona fide relic of the days when ox teams dragged huge redwood logs to the dozen mills in the vicinity and lumber from the mills to the Embarcadero. The store was a center for Saturday night celebrations that must have approached the riot level, as well as serving during the week for the more prosaic commercial needs of the surrounding community.

According to the San Mateo County Parks & Recreation Department, which has administered the site since 1947, this is the second store building erected there, dating from 1854. Originally it was known as Tripp's Store, later as the Woodside Family Grocery.

(The site was closed to the public for a time in 1979-80, a victim of Proposition 13, but was reopened by the San Mateo County Historical Association in September, 1980, three days a week—Sunday, Monday, and Wednesday).

The store was built and operated by Mathias Parkhurst and Dr. Orville Tripp, who were partners in a shingle mill near the present-day village of Woodside, starting about 1849. Tripp, a dentist from Massachusetts, found both the climate and the ethical standards of his fellow practitioners in San Francisco too much to tolerate. He joined Parkhurst, about whom little seems to be known, and turned to hauling logs by ox team down to the bay shore where they could be floated on the outgoing tide to San Francisco.

As more and more mills sprang up in the vicinity, the two partners decided a store would be an easier way to make a living. They started with a crude lean-to in 1851, then built the present store across the road three years later, supplying not only groceries but liquor (without benefit of license) to the hungry and thirsty lumberjacks, who numbered upward of a thousand.

The new community soon acquired a temperance hall, for all the good it did. The store became a U.S. post office with Parkhurst as postmaster. Tripp doubled as dentist for the bustling place. Having the only armored safe anywhere around, the store also served as the community bank, and the partners as the bankers. A library was organized in 1859. Tripp also served on San Francisco's first Board of Supervisors, in 1851. In 1856 he married Miss Emeline Skellton, also from Massachusetts, who had answered the bachelor partners' advertisement for a housekeeper. Tripp built a home across the road for himself and his wife.

Although the mills closed when the logging activity moved west of the summit after the 1860s, the store continued to prosper as agriculture developed in the valley. Several vineyards were by then producing wine grapes, and Tripp was quick to cash in on the new source of revenue. He built a winery next door to the store and marketed his own brand, "The San Mateo County Pioneer."

Parkhurst died in 1863, at the age of 34, and Tripp carried on until his death in 1909, when the store closed. The building was occupied as a home by Tripp's only child, Adele, until her death in 1926. For a time it was used as a church, then was purchased by the county in 1940 and renovated. Built entirely of redwood, the structure required only minor repairs. Residents of the region helped to collect much of the original equipment and furnishings to create a local museum. It became an official county historical site in 1947 upon the recommendation of the county historical society. It is also an official California state historical landmark.

The sprawling village of Woodside today incorporates what is left of the community that was served by the store; another settlement known as Whiskey Hill because it had three saloons; and a cluster of houses called Greersburg, named for the early-day Greer family who then owned the Rancho Canada de Raymundo.

A few miles south, near the junction of Woodside Road with Sand Hill Road on the Stanford Campus, lies another ghost of a ghost town

Woodside Store, west of present-day Woodside Village, is a relic of logging days.

that was a booming center of activity in the logging days. It is now under Searsville Lake, a part of Stanford's water supply.

Searsville grew up around the home of John H. Sears, who came around the Horn to California in 1849. His house became a hotel known as the Sears House, serving as a rest stop for the teams hauling lumber out of the hills to Redwood City. A lively meeting place on Sundays, the little community was doomed by the construction of the Searsville Dam in the 1890s. A schoolhouse on a hill overlooking the lake survived the flood, but succumbed to a lack of attendance in 1893 and later was torn down. A plaque near the shore of Searsville Lake now designates the old town site an official California historical landmark.

It was while driving stage between Searsville and Redwood City in 1858 that the celebrated driver named Charley Parkhurst was kicked in the face by a horse. The injury cost Charley an eye and a severely deformed jaw, both contributing to Charley's disguise as a man. It was not known until her death near Soquel in 1879 that she was a woman. Charley was no relation to storekeeper Parkhurst.

Perhaps the only public record of Charley's career appeared in 1866, when she was listed in the great register of voters in Santa Cruz County and actually voted in the election of November 3, 1868. It was the first time in American history that a woman was known to have voted in a public election.

New Almaden

In early spring, if winter rains have been generous, the hillsides turn to green velvet and myriads of wildflowers spread over the land. The creeks run and the reservoirs fill and cattle grow sleek. For a brief spell the scene becomes one of rare beauty, but by the end of summer the hills have turned golden brown again and there is little to catch the eye.

It is like that in the Santa Teresa hills, an eastern spur of the Santa Cruz Mountains a dozen miles south of San Jose, just as it is in most of California below the snow line. In these rocky hills, the locale of Almaden Quicksilver County Park, it is hard to imagine any enterprise more ambitious than raising goats ever could have flourished. Certainly there is little to suggest the unique and vital role the region played in the nation's history.

To the casual eye, this relatively new and undeveloped county recreation area, covering 3,570 acres of hillside and canyon, looks barren, even formidable, most of the time. But then, old mines are seldom noted for their beauty. Environmental impact were not words of any potency when these mines were established a long time ago, and the impact of mines on the landscape was little short of a disaster.

A couple of small reservoirs open to fishing and boating when there is water in them, some 30 miles of riding and hiking trails, parking space, a picnic area with restrooms and barbecue pits—these are about all the facilities offered by the park so far.

Civilization nowadays is limited to the tiny village of New Almaden, just outside the southeastern edge of the park. Here may be found Casa Grande (Big House), center of activity for more than a century. There are also a gaggle of rustic cottages, a post office, a restaurant, a scattering of contemporary homes—but no motel, no trailer park.

Under the surface, quite literally, there is more, very much more, as a visit to the excellent little New Almaden Museum (privately owned and operated) on the main street of the village will reveal.

Here the visitor will find how it was that this once was the richest and most important mine in all of California. The San Jose historian Clyde Arbuckle has listed five facts to support that contention:

1. Almaden was the first producing quicksilver mine in all of North America.

2. It was the first mine of any consequence in California, having been discovered 27 months before the Coloma gold strike.

3. It was the state's richest single mine ever, having produced at least $70 million in quicksilver. (The only gold or silver mines that exceeded that output were clusters of mines).

4. It broke an international monopoly that would have crippled the Gold Rush. (At the time, quicksilver was required in large amounts for recovering gold and silver from ore, but nearly all of it then came from Spain's ancient Almaden mines.)

5. It helped to keep California and Nevada in the Union and thus to finance the Union cause in the Civil War. (During the war, unscrupulous New York financiers persuaded President Lincoln to order the mines seized by federal troops, an action that would have tipped those two states into the Confederacy. At the last minute, Lincoln rescinded the order.)

The name New Almaden is of obvious origin, taking after its Spanish rival, but the county park, established in 1975, is called simply Almaden Quicksilver. About half of it has been registered as a national historical landmark district.

Some maps show the village of New Almaden as Hacienda, although the post office has operated since 1861 either as Almaden or New Almaden. At the peak of the operation two other villages supported the mines Mexican Camp and English Camp, both on Mine Hill, of which little now remains.

The park takes in all or part of several other, smaller quicksilver mines nearby, such as Senator, Enriquita, Randol, and some of the Guadalupe workings.

Although the hills are honeycombed with more than 100 miles of underground tunnels and shafts, the deepest reaching nearly 2,500 feet down, there is little surface evidence of that activity today. A couple of massive concrete structures still stand at the Senator Mine, at the end of the road just beyond the temporary park office on McAbee Road. At the village of New Almaden, parts of two brick ducts may be seen slanting up the side of Mine Hill to the chimneys at the top—all that remains of the original reduction works.

It used to be possible for adventurous folks to prowl all over the ruins of the mines—when they were not in production—and to scare themselves silly by exploring the deep tunnels, listening to the creaking and groaning of the roof timbers.

So much timber had to be used to shore up the roofs and walls in this treacherous terrain only a few miles from the San Andreas earthquake fault—it is small wonder that the hills for many miles around were denuded of their trees and still are.

Because the area has become a county park, however, the county does not want the responsibility for the consequences of having a citizen (or even a tourist) fall down one of the open shafts, an experience said to be injurious to the health.

Lacking the funds to safeguard a dozen or more such openings, the county has put Mine Hill out of bounds and fenced off the roads leading to it, thereby removing from public access probably the most interesting part of the park. Barring a large donation, or the repeal of Proposition 13, the situation does not appear likely to change very soon.

Long ago the brick smelters and their tall chimneys were dismantled and hauled away for building materials, or ground up as a source of quicksilver absorbed during the long periods of active use. Time, weather, and vandals have completed the destruction, leaving only the adobe buildings in the village of New Almaden intact.

It is certainly no exaggeration to state that the quicksilver produced by New Almaden from 1848 until the early 1890s helped to make the California Gold Rush what it was, but the statement needs some background.

Quicksilver furnaces at New Almaden, circa 1880s. (Winn-Bulmore)

The presence of the dark red mercury ore called cinnabar in the Santa Teresa hills was well known to the Indians of the Santa Clara Valley. Tribes from British Columbia to Mexico traded for the bright red clay they used for facial adornment. Arrowheads found in considerable numbers indicate that battles were fought for possession of what was known as Red Cave. There early Spanish explorers found holes 40 to 50 feet deep where the natives had mined their *moketka*, or red earth.

A Spanish settler named Antonio Suñol tried to extract gold and silver from the ore as early as 1828. But it was not until 1845 that it came to the attention of a more knowledgeable individual, a Captain Andres Castillero of the Mexican Army.

Castillero conducted a crude experiment by heating some cinnabar in a flask and allowing the vapor to condense, thus producing a few drops of that oddest of elements—liquid metal called quicksilver, or mercury.

Both gold and silver happily amalgamate with quicksilver in a method known for centuries. In Mexico as late as the turn of this century, blindfolded mules dragged boulders or huge stone wheels around and around a pile of crushed ore mixed with quicksilver to create the amalgam.

After the quicksilver had done its magical work in gathering up the gold and silver, it was easily driven off by heat in retorts or smelters, freeing the more precious metals. The early methods and machines used in this part of the process were crude, so that while it was possible to recapture the mercury by cooling and condensation, in actual practice most of it went up the chimney or out through the cracks—incidentally contributing nothing helpful to the environment.

Castillero had good reason to be interested in the result of his experiment. Cut off from its supply from Spain after the Mexican revolution of 1823, the Mexican government was offering a reward of $100,000 for a quicksilver strike. His discovery was also just in time for the California Gold Rush.

Once the streams of the Mother Lode country had been stripped of their available gold nuggets and heavy gold-bearing sands, which could be readily panned for pay dirt, miners were forced to try to wrest the precious metal from solid rock. This took a lot of back-breaking pick-and-shovel work, later assisted by blasting.

Then came hydraulic mining, using streams of high pressure water to tear down whole hillsides and to fill the lower valleys with mountains of gravel. Enormous stamp mills were set up at the cost of incredible labor and expense to crush the ore. Before the days of industrial steel, all the machinery was made of cast iron, using bulk for strength. The result was equipment of vast size and weight.

But the end result was the same. Out came a mess of pulverized gravel and sand intermixed with gold and silver and assorted other heavy elements, extremely difficult to separate. Quicksilver from the mines at New Almaden contributed the crucial element needed by the miners to continue to extract gold from California's ore. Without New Almaden, the Gold Rush would have been dependent upon Mexico for its supply of mercury.

Then in the 1890s a new method employing cyanide instead of mercury for recovering gold and silver from crushed ore came into use, a method vastly cheaper and more efficient than the mercury process. The price of quicksilver dropped sharply.

However, there are many other uses for quicksilver in paints and pigments, in medicine, in electronic components and electrical switches, in chemistry, arc lights, and explosives, to name but a few.

So New Almaden continued to produce quicksilver on a diminishing scale off and on until about a decade ago. The peak of employment was in 1864–65, when there were 1,112 men on the payroll and the population of the district numbered more than 5,000. In 1865 New Almaden's production exceeded that of its Spanish namesake (which has been in continuous production since Roman times) and did so for the ensuing 50-odd years.

The area became a park rather suddenly when in June 1973 the county learned that the owner, the New Idria Mining & Chemical Company (Herbert Hoover's one-time concern), was planning to auction off the land. Using its park acquisition funds and a matching federal grant, the county bought the first six of nine parcels for $2,000,000 and took an option on the rest.

The new park was formally dedicated May 19, 1974. Meanwhile the company continued limited operations on the rest of the property until 1966, when all mining activity ceased. The county had picked up its option on the last three parcels for $1,500,000 in 1975, leasing it in part to the company for the final year.

Since Mine Hill with its relics of two towns—English Town and Mexican Camp and a dozen or so shafts is out of bounds for now, about all there is to see in the way of historic interest is some rows of tall, dark Italian cypress trees marking the location of the three cemeteries. All three have long since been robbed of their tombstones, a sad requiem for a once-bustling community of several thousand souls.

Stevens Creek County Park

Stevens Creek County Park shares with Mt. Madonna County Park the honor of being the oldest in the Santa Clara County park system, both dating from 1926-27. The most accessible of all the foothill and mountain parks around San Jose, it contains some surprising features not well known to its hordes of visitors.

At a glance Stevens Creek might seem to belong more to the valley than to the mountains, since it is bounded on two sides by the city limits of Cupertino, but its tanglewood interior rises sharply to the respectable elevation of 1,600 feet. In its upper reaches it is unquestionably mountainous and in some areas quite wild and inaccessible.

As its name implies, the 685-acre park lies along, and is named for, a stream called Stevens Creek, which runs into the Bay beyond Mountain View. It incorporates Stevens Creek Reservoir, an old water conservation lake no longer in full use. Stevens Canyon Road, its main access route off the Foothill Expressway, becomes Mt. Eden Road farther up the line, connecting in turn with Pierce Road, which leads on up to Highway 9 above Saratoga.

Because of its close proximity to San Jose, and its varied attractions, it has long been one of the county's most heavily used parks, especially in summer. Attendance peaked at 1.2 million per year in the early 1970s, but dropped to about 750,000 per year after 1976 when the reservoir's water level had to be lowered to meet modem earthquake standards.

When the dam, a rolled-earth type, was built in 1935, it was not known that it virtually straddled a branch of the great San Andreas earthquake fault. The dam stands 120 feet high, and is 1,000 feet long on the crest. At full capacity, the 93-acre lake holds 3,970 acre-feet of water, but as a safety measure it is not allowed to rise above about one-third of that level.

The reservoir is still used, on a much smaller scale than formerly, for fishing and non-power boating, as well as for flood control in the rainy season. Incidentally, the reservoir once had to be drained entirely, not long after it was built. Fishermen reported that huge goldfish, or Japanese carp, were devouring all the trout and other planted game fish. Subsequently it was discovered that a large goldfish pond on a private estate in the hills had been washed out in a flash flood, sending numerous big carp down to the lake. Only by draining it dry could the carp and other trash fish be eliminated.

Nowadays the park offers year-around daytime escape from the hurly-burly of metropolitan San Jose in its several shady picnic areas, hiking and nature trails, horseback riding, a natural history lecture series in summer, an archery range, and some small stream fishing on occasion. There are no overnight facilities.

The park is connected by trail to Fremont Older Open Space Preserve adjoining its eastern boundary. As yet it has no road or trail connection with Upper Stevens Creek County Park, an entirely undeveloped tract that runs on up to the Skyline Boulevard.

The park's history is relatively brief, since the region was not involved in early Spanish or Mexican grants. Before the turn of the century most of the area was used for hunting, fishing and some fur-trapping. Later, there were wineries in the lower foothills, followed by quarries such as the present-day Kaiser Permanente plant, which the park adjoins on the west.

The creek running through the park was named for Elisha Stevens, an early American adventurer who came overland with a wagon train several years before the Gold Rush. In the 1850s he took up government land for a homestead along the creek below the park.

Although a fire destroyed many of the church records in 1910, leaving a blank in the detailed history of the region, it is known that much of the present park property was owned by the Jesuits at the University of Santa Clara. They operated, among many enterprises, a four-story winery which was built in 1875. It burned down in 1969. Back in the 1880s it was one of the University's chief resources, having produced as much as $10,000 in wine in a single year.

A man named Ray Byron bought a portion of the property from the Jesuits in 1945 with the avowed intention of subdividing it for residences, but the plan fell through and he sold out to Kaiser.

The lower portion of the park, around the entrance, was known as the Villa Maria when it was owned by the Jesuits. It served not only as a profitable farm, including the big winery, but also as a retreat for the Jesuit fathers from the University. It became part of the park in the early 1970s after the Jesuits decided not to rebuild the winery.

One of the most fascinating aspects of the park, at least to naturalists and horticulturists, is a small grove of about 30 American chestnut trees *(Castanea dentata)*, related to the common horse chestnut but a native of the eastern United States. Once one of the dominant hardwood trees of the eastern forests, it provided food and lumber on a vast scale before it was all but wiped out by an invasion of Asiatic fungus about 1904–06. Similar to the Dutch elm bark infection, the disease killed almost all of the mature American chestnuts, and by 1940 the tree was no longer listed in most American tree books.

For decades great ghost forests of dead chestnuts provided fuel, lumber, and tannin. The tree is still cultivated as an ornamental shrub but rarely attains tree size except in Stevens Creek County Park. Most of the chestnuts sold on the American market in modern times have come from Europe.

The park grove, planted about 1890 by the Jesuits, has unaccountably managed to escape the plague. It may well be the only grove of its kind west of the Mississippi, or anywhere else.

Felton

Ιt seems a shame that the town of Felton, nine miles up the San Lorenzo River valley from Monterey Bay, has such an uninspired name, especially since it is surrounded by places with such mellifluous designations as Santa Cruz, Bonny Doon, Lompico, and Zayante.

For all its hectic downtown traffic and its gaggle of tourist-type stores, Felton's attractions are many and varied, its history rich in regional lore dating from Spanish times. But it was named, more than a century ago, by a man who was more interested in honoring a friend than he was in musical-sounding words, or history.

George Treat, one of the Yankee purchasers of the big Mexican land grant called Rancho Zayante, simply named the town for a close friend and attorney when he laid out the town site in 1878. The honored friend was Charles N. Felton, an attorney lately from New York. Later, Felton became active in state politics, serving as an assemblyman (1880–81), member of Congress (1885–89), U.S. Senator (1891–93), and as a member of the State Board of Prison Directors (1903–07). He made his home on the other side of the mountains, between Atherton and Menlo Park. So much for the name.

Of course, at the time George Treat could have had no remote idea of what lay in the future for his tiny town, which in those early days did not even have a bridge over the San Lorenzo River. It was connected with Santa Cruz and the outside world only by a muddy and rocky wagon road and the narrow-gauge railroad completed two years earlier. Even before it was a town, Felton was an important shipping point for lime, lumber, and shingles and remained so until automobiles and trucks and paved highways changed the face of the land and the habits of people, half a century later.

Nowadays Felton is both a busy tourist center and a bedroom suburb of Santa Cruz. It has not one railroad but two, in a manner of speaking, although one carries only sand and the other one goes around in a circle. Here are some of the principal places of interest in and around the town:

Henry Cowell State Redwood Park in two sections, one northwest and one southeast of the town, both bordering on the fringes of the community and inseparable from it.

Felton covered bridge, dating from 1892, the highest covered bridge in the nation, and the only remaining one made of redwood.

Mt. Hermon, a Christian religious retreat and conference center since 1905. It is named, rather ambitiously, for a peak in Lebanon (Jabel Ash Shaykh) which is 9,232 feet high. The local Mt. Hermon is a wooded knob only 410 feet above sea level, 120 feet higher than neighboring Felton. Lost in a cluster of cabins is the unmarked site of California's first power sawmill, built in 1842 by the redoubtable Isaac Graham.

Also unmarked is the site, in the southern part of town, of the lower terminus of the spectacular San Lorenzo Valley flume, an elevated V-shaped trough that carried lumber from the vicinity of Boulder Creek to the railhead at Felton in the 1880s.

In addition to its logging railroad, which extended as far as Boulder Creek from 1884 until 1934, Felton was the junction point of the South Pacific Company's passenger and freight service over the mountains from 1880 until 1940. Part of this historic and scenic line, convened to standard gauge by the Southern Pacific in 1907, still operates as a freight carrier through Santa Cruz from a sand quarry near Olympia. The line crosses the San Lorenzo on an old steel bridge in the middle of Henry Cowell State Redwood Park, just south of the old Big Trees station, and follows on down the west bank of the riven

Local rail buffs have long proposed rebuilding the line to Los Gatos as an energy-saving alternative to the perpetually crowded Highway 17, but there would seem to be little chance of this ever taking place. For one thing, all the old bridges and trestles are gone and the tunnels blasted shut from Olympia to Los Gatos. For another, the Santa Cruz city and county governments are opposed to any further development of their territory as a bedroom for San Jose.

Paved highways and side roads lead in all directions out of Felton, which in summer becomes a highly congested multiple crossroads. The principal route is State Highway 9, main road out of Santa Cruz and up the San Lorenzo Valley through a string of residential resort communities. This is also the main route to Big Basin State Park, and to the summit where it connects with Skyline Boulevard. It is still only a two-lane road with narrow bridges and sharp curves throughout.

Graham Hill Road, a good alternative route to Santa Cruz, skirts the southern section of Henry Cowell Redwoods State Park on its eastern edge, then becomes Ocean Avenue in downtown Santa Cruz, also serving as the road access to the park's only campground.

East Zayante Road dips under Mt. Hermon Road to thread its way through the narrow canyons and gulches that contain the sidehill residential suburbs of Zayante, Olympia, and Lompico. Beyond Lompico, at an elevation of 580 feet above sea level, is beautiful Loch Lomond Reservoir, formerly called Newell Lake. It is a day-use recreation facility of the city of Santa Cruz.

East Zayante Road continues, at least on the maps, all the way to Summit Road, following an old ox route used for hauling timber from the upper Zayante drainage a century or so ago. But it is at best a jeep track, often impassable, in its upper reaches.

Westward out of downtown Felton the narrow, steep and crooked Felton-Empire Road leads up to Bonny Doon past the undeveloped Fall Creek section of Henry Cowell Redwoods State Park. On Bonny Doon ridge it joins Empire Grade and Pine Flat Road before going on down the western slope to the coast as Davenport, under the name of Bonny Doon Road. Bonny Doon, once the center of a flourishing lumber industry, lies as an elevation or 800 feet. Even its post office has been moved to Davenport, leaving only a combination bar and store to distinguish it as a community.

Felton's principal highway to the east is called Mt. Hermon Road, although it no longer goes to Mt. Hermon. It swings through the sand hills to the town of Scott's Valley, four miles eastward, where it joins Highway 17 and other roads.

Covered Bridges

Santa Cruz County has the most covered bridges still standing of any county in the state, all of them deep enough in the hills to be considered part of the mountain picture.

To be sure, the total number is only three (or 3½ if you count the pigmy built in recent years as a commercial tourist attraction at Felton). There are counties in Oregon and Washington that still have dozens of these quaint relics, but even three are not to be sneezed at any more. According to Kramer Adams, the Western authority on the subject, covered bridges, which once numbered more than a thousand in the western states, are disappearing at the rate of about ten a year.

Thus the trio in Santa Cruz County, all well preserved and unlikely to be discarded, have attained considerable historical importance and doubtless will continue to enjoy that status for a long time to come.

Why covered bridges? In the days of steel-tired wagons and steel-shod horses, before rubber tires and asphalt roads, the wooden flooring of timber bridges took a terrible beating, especially in regions of heavy precipitation. To protect the flooring and main supports from rain, fog, and snow, bridges were commonly roofed over and siding added, until the innovation of modern chemical wood preservatives, concrete bridges, and paved highways. Some railroad bridges had the siding without the roofs, giving them an upside-down appearance.

The Felton Bridge, over the San Lorenzo River just south of the town's main highway intersection, is said to be the last one of its kind built of redwood. It is also said to be the highest or tallest in the United States, but why it was designed that way remains a mystery.

When it was taken out of active service in 1929 to become an historical landmark (California no. 583), it became the first western example of the custom of preserving by-passed bridges, according to Kramer Adams.

Erected in 1892, the Felton Bridge is 180 feet long. It replaced an earlier open structure put up in 1878 after repeated petitioning by Felton residents. Although the road up the San Lorenzo to Felton from Santa Cruz had been completed in 1868, residents and travelers alike had to ford the river, when the water was low enough, for a decade. When the river was high, horses had to swim with mail, passengers, even with supplies for the first hotel, Bib Tree House. The hotel was erected early in 1878 by Mr. and Mrs. George Day, who also operated a livery stable and stage line.

The Felton Bridge is one of the best known in the state because of its accessibility. It is maintained by funds raised by the citizens in a yearly pancake breakfast staged by the volunteer fire department. The event carries on a tradition that started back in the 1860s when an old-time costume ball was held in Santa Cruz to raise money for the original bridge.

A few miles downstream from Felton the Paradise Park covered bridge spans the river in the summer home colony of the Masonic Lodge, which adjoins the southern edge of Henry Cowell Park. It is the only covered bridge in the county still used daily for both pedestrians and vehicles, and is the only one in the west protected at both ends by fire hoses.

The Masonic Park is on the site of an early-day sawmill, and the first paper pulp mill in California. The pulp mill ran only from 1860 until 1862, when a flood wrecked the flume that supplied water to the operation. Three years later the California Powder Works built a plant on the same site to make blasting powder for the new Central Pacific Railroad's construction. Its grinding wheels were driven by water from a 1,300-foot tunnel that tapped the river farther upstream.

Dupont took over the powder company, which had produced the world's first smokeless powder, and shut down the plant in 1916, leaving only the tunnel, some foundations and the name Powder Mill Flat for history to recall, besides the covered bridge.

Built in 1872 to carry a railroad as well as wagon traffic to and from the powder mill, this 180-foot span was intended to last. A new tin roof and an occasional coat of paint have served to keep it in good repair ever since the railroad tracks were removed during World War I.

Because of its attractive setting over a creek, the Glen Canyon Covered Bridge has appeared in many movies and TV shows. Only 83 feet long, it was moved all in a piece from its original site on Glen Canyon Road in 1939, when it was only 47 years old but about ready to fall down. On its new location half a block away in DeLaveaga City Park, it has been refurbished and its board siding removed the latter because the city fathers thought the enclosed bridge might be used for some illicit pursuits.

Glen Canyon Bridge is the southernmost covered bridge in California, and the only one within the Santa Cruz city limits that is still standing. It is open only for pedestrian use in the park.

Ben Lomond, Brookdale, Boulder Creek

The three little highway towns above Felton on the San Lorenzo River—Ben Lomond, Brookdale, and Boulder Creek—all had their origins in the logging woods and lumber mills that provided most of the jobs in the latter part of the 19th century.

Ben Lomond, largest of the present-day communities, started out in life as Pacific Mills. According to Leon Rowland it was named for the big lumber operation of James P. Pierce's Pacific Manufacturing Company which dated from the late 1870s.

But the U.S. Post Office Department insisted on changing the name for some reason, and after a bit of arguing with the citizens the local post office became officially Ben Lomond, after the long mountain that overlooks the town. A year later, in 1888, the town site was laid out by Pierce and Associates.

Among the earliest settlers, preceding the mill and the town by a couple of decades, was Harry Love, a veteran of the Mexican War who was known as "The Black Knight of Zayante" because of his flowing hair style and fancy dress. Love was leader of the rangers who hunted down and killed Joaquin Murietta, the notorious Mexican bandit. Love was paid $5,000 by a grateful state legislature for his deed (a tidy sum in those days), which enabled him to acquire a logging operation and a water-powered sawmill, and to build a road to Felton called Love Grade. The creek that ran by the mill was named Love Creek, one of several that join the San Lorenzo River in and around the town. Love later was killed in a shooting scrape in Santa Clara.

Tourists and weekenders arrived with the railroad in 1884, soon converting the lumber village to one of summer cabins. The big Rowardennan Hotel became a popular mountain resort served by the railroad. Jim Jeffries, the great heavyweight prizefighter, is said to have trained there for his last fight.

Ben Lomond is now a busy crossroads, with routes leading off via Glen Arbor and Quail Hollow roads to Olympia, Zayante and Loch Lomond Reservoir to the east; and via Alba Road to Empire Grade and Ben Lomond Mountain to the west. Highland County Park, a day-use recreation facility, is a mile south of town on Highway 9.

Brookdale, not much more that a wide place in the highway with a large resort hotel/motel (Brookdale Inn) on one side, lies so close to Boulder Creek it seemed destined to be absorbed by its larger neighbor to the north one of these days.

Twenty-five or so years ago Brookdale was world-famous for its Brookdale Lodge, built in 1923 over Clear Creek, which ran merrily right through the dining room, lending a musical accompaniment to the clatter of the cutlery and the chatter of the customers. Alas, the Lodge burned down in 1956. Its site adjoins present-day Brookdale Inn, which started out as an annex to the Lodge.

Brookdale also was the early-day home of John Logan, who gave his name to a hybrid blackberry/raspberry cross he developed in his Santa Cruz garden after he became a superior judge there. While living in what was to become Brookdale, Logan built a small hotel (predecessor of the Lodge), sold lots in the town he laid out in 1900, and was credited with having brought a state fish hatchery to town.

At first, the settlement was called Reed's Spur, then Clear Creek, finally Brookdale after the post office was established under that name in 1902. The area had been logged over by various operators in the 1870s and 1880s, then, like its neighbors, the tiny village became a mecca for weekend and summer visitors after the railroad arrived in 1884.

Boulder Creek, 13 miles up the San Lorenzo River, is a lively resort center with a variety of business that thrives on the seasonal tourist trade. Anyone passing through there today, even on a hectic holiday weekend, would have difficulty, however, in imagining that it once supported sixteen saloons catering to the hordes of thirsty lumberjacks from the dozens of logging camps and sawmills operating at the turn of the century. Saturday nights must have been wild indeed.

Boulder Creek was busy enough even as far back as 1867, when the county supervisors deemed it necessary to authorize the building of a road up from Napoleon Bonaparte Hicks's place (later to become Ben Lomond) to "the forks of the San Lorenzo." The construction in 1875 of the 13-mile San Lorenzo Valley flume to bring lumber down to the railhead at Felton from a point five miles above Boulder Creek opened up additional logging areas and the town boomed.

Finally, the railroad (narrow-gauge until 1907) arrived in 1883, and Boulder Creek soon became one of the busiest lumber shipping points in the state. The flume was torn down south of the town but continued in use above there for a few more years.

All this activity served to settle the fate of a rival community, called Lorenzo, a mile or so south of Boulder Creek, which had been laid out in 1875 by Joseph W. Peery, first postmaster at Boulder Creek. When the railroad arrived, it needed a site for its terminal. Peery let greed get ahead of good judgement and asked so high a price for his property that the railroad instead chose a site farther north in Boulder Creek.

The railroad continued to carry freight and passengers up the valley until it ran out of business, between the depression and competition from gas buggies, in 1934. The tracks were torn up as far as Felton, and Boulder Creek became strictly a highway town.

Lorenzo, in the meantime, was all but obliterated by a fire in 1897. Although Peery rebuilt his hotel there, the town never recovered and eventually was absorbed entirely by Boulder Creek. Boulder Creek had its disastrous fires, too—one in 1891 burned the hotel, six saloons, and half a dozen stores, but the town was soon rebuilt. There never was any shortage of lumber there.

Situated at the junction of several forks of the San Lorenzo River (including the one for which the town is named) Boulder Creek is the jumping-off place for the throngs of visitors to Big Basin Redwoods State Park. Highway 236, main access route to the park, joins Highway 9 in the middle of town.

At the town's northern edge, Bear Creek Road branches off to the east to join the Skyline Boulevard (Summit Road) above Lexington Reservoir. Originally a toll road built in 1875, it never paid its own way and was acquired by the county in 1890–91.

Several church camps and Boy Scout and Girl Scout camps are situated just outside the town on Highway 9 and some of its tributary roads.

Index